SAVORING THE SEASONS

RIVERSIDE

New Bern, North Carolina

**THE BOSCH COMPANIES
OF NEW BERN**

B/S/H/ Home Appliance Corp.

 BOSCH

$\mathcal{S}$AVORING THE $\mathcal{S}$EASONS: RIVERSIDE
Copyright © 2000
The Craven Regional Medical Center Foundation
233 Middle Street, Suite 208
New Bern, North Carolina 28560
or
P.O. Box 12157
New Bern, North Carolina 28561
252-633-8247

Library of Congress Number: 00-133364
ISBN: 0-9701460-0-0

Designed, Edited, and Manufactured by
Favorite Recipes® Press
An imprint of

FRP™

P. O. Box 305142
Nashville, Tennessee 37230
1-800-358-0560

Art Director: Steve Newman
Book Design: Starletta Polster
Project Manager: Susan Larson

Manufactured in the United States of America
First Printing: 2000   5,000 copies

TABLE OF CONTENTS

PREFACE
page 4

ACKNOWLEDGMENTS
page 6

MISSION STATEMENT
page 7

INTRODUCTION
page 8

WHEN SPRING IS IN THE AIR
page 9

A SULTRY SUMMER DAY
page 61

DURING THE AUTUMN MONTHS
page 105

ON A WINTER'S NIGHT
page 157

A HISTORY OF CARING
page 198

CONTRIBUTORS LIST
page 200

INDEX
page 202

ORDER INFORMATION
page 208

PREFACE

Dear Cookbook Patron:

Every organization has its own history to record and pass on to future generations who one day may drive its growth and shape its future. And so it is with the Craven Regional Medical Center Foundation. Although its history is brief, its accomplishments are broad.

Organized in 1996 by the Craven Regional Medical Center Board of Commissioners, with its own bylaws, board of directors, and a mission to serve the three-county area, it was led by Kenneth Morris as the first board president. Several of the founding members of the board still continue at its helm today, including J. Closs Barker, our current president, John Haroldson, chairman of our Allocations and Disbursement Committee, and Joe Austin and Kenneth Morris, past presidents.

In 1996 and 1997, Medical Center employees and members of the medical staff kicked off the Foundation's initial fund-raising effort, with the employees raising funds for a solarium space on the fourth southeast floor of the hospital to be enjoyed by patients, families, and employees alike. Physicians began important funds such as Cancer Care and Community Health, which are still contributing dollars for critical health care needs in our community today.

Our second president, Joe Austin, of Ward and Smith, P.A., led the Foundation to the completion of its first full year of campaigning and the establishment of the Allocations and Disbursements Committee, which responsibly reviews applications from area nonprofits wishing to implement projects or programs having a direct impact on the health of the community.

In 1998 Norman Kellum, of the Kellum Law Firm, began a two-year commitment as president of the Foundation, leading it through its first capital campaign, "Building a Safe Harbor," so capably chaired by Troy Smith, and two full years of strong partnerships with area nonprofits such as the Craven County Health Department, the MERCI and HOPE Free Clinics, and the Craven County Council on Women. During Mr. Kellum's tenure, the Foundation assumed its position as a charitable entity in New Bern, forging donor relationships with more than 1,000 families, individuals, and businesses.

As the Foundation moves into its fourth year, having completed the $300,000 "Building A Safe Harbor" campaign for the CRMC's Oncology Center addition, and having made allocations of $161,000 to area nonprofits during the past two years, it faces its future full of hope that more will be achieved in the years to come, more people will be helped, and greater differences will be made in people's lives. With your purchase of *Savoring the Seasons: Riverside*, you help the Foundation achieve these goals. We thank you.

Sincerely,

J. Closs Barker

President

Margaret D. Shields

Executive Director

ACKNOWLEDGMENTS

*This book would not have been possible without the hard work and dedication
of the following employees and Foundation board members,
who have faithfully served on the cookbook committee for the past year.*

Joni Battersby
Lila Cotten
Loretta Croscutt
Teri Duckworth
Lisa Edwards, Chairperson & Employee Sales
Cathy Garvick
Dawn Jenkins
Megan McGarvey
Bettina Meekins, M.D., Honorary Chairperson
Leslie Pittman
Margaret Shields
Scott Smith
Alice Underhill, Cookbook Advisor

*Acknowledgments and Special Appreciation to the following members of the community who
volunteered their time to make this book come alive in pictures and prose:*

Members of the Tryon Palace Staff:
Hilliary Hicks, Historian
Michelle Rafoon, Public Relations
Shirley Willis, Domestication

Nora Barden
Leah Bell
Bill Benners, Photographer
Craven County Convention & Visitors Bureau
Craven County Public Library
Craven-Jones-Pamlico Medical Alliance
The Dunes Club
Employees of Craven Regional Medical Center
Lynn Everett

Ann Griggs, Floral Designer
Betsy Hathaway
Steve Hicks
The Lancing House
Phyllis Owens
Wright Shields, M.D.
Mary Silver
Swiss Bear
Alice Underhill
Mr. and Mrs. John P. Weyerhaeuser IV

MISSION STATEMENT

CRAVEN REGIONAL MEDICAL CENTER FOUNDATION

*The mission of the
Craven Regional Medical Center Foundation
is to complement the medical services
provided by Craven Regional Medical Center
and other nonprofit medical service providers; and to
improve the overall health of the community
through the development of financial resources,
including public and private funding sources,
and the financial management of these resources.*

SPONSORS

Gold Sponsors
The Bosch Companies of New Bern
S-B Power Tools
BSH Home Appliances

Silver Sponsors
Weyerhaeuser Real Estate
Coldwell Banker Willis-Smith Company
Roche Pharmaceuticals

Bronze Sponsors
Bank of America
Benners Studio, Incorporated
Coastal Carolina Health Care
Chesnutt, Clemmons, Thomas & Peacock, P.A.
Coastal Eye Clinic and Laser Vision Center
Hampton Inn
Hatteras Yachts, A Division of Gen-Mar
Jenkins Gas & Oil Company
Kenneth Morris Insurance

INTRODUCTION

New Bern, North Carolina

Where the history of this small coastal city that transcends time begins....

Once the capital of Colonial North Carolina and a major port for shipping during that period in North Carolina history, New Bern stands at the confluence of the Trent and Neuse Rivers, which provide the city with its unique coastal heritage—a heritage that runs as deep as the rivers' channels and byways.

These rivers are an integral part of New Bern's life, their waters constantly ebbing and flowing with the shifting winds and storms. Over the years, New Bern's people have derived their customs, their trade, and their pleasure from these waters and the bounty they offer to coastal inhabitants. As the seasons passed, New Bern evolved from Colonial Capital of North Carolina to an occupied Confederate port during the Civil War.

During the post–Civil War period, as the South became more industrialized, men worked in factories and on ships rather than on the family farm. The large midday meal was replaced with dinner in the evening, and there was greater access to fresh produce, with local shops on Craven and Middle Streets carrying products arriving by train and steamship.

New Bern's rivers were highways for the lumber industry. More pine lumber was shipped out of New Bern during its shipping heyday in the late 1800s and early 1900s than any other Atlantic port. Three- and four-masted schooners loaded with lumber were towed by towboat through the bridge and out into the Neuse River.

Despite its reputation as "The Athens of North Carolina" as its shipping and lumber business flourished, New Bern kept its neighborhood charm with the historic downtown sections: Ghent, Riverside, Duffyfield, and James City. *An Oral History of New Bern* recalls that downtown there was a "mix of families," rich, middle-class and poor; black and white. "Neighborhoods have the strangest way of changing sizes—to children they seem so big; years later they seem so small. Remembered, they seem magical."

New Bern's historic homes perched on the water's edge serve as reminders of generations that laughed and sang to entertain one another around their fireplaces and on their back porches. Neighborhoods still congregate in backyards, on porches, docks, and around bonfires to savor the seasons. Entertaining friends and family continues to be an integral part of life in this small southern city.

In *Savoring the Seasons: Riverside*, we give to you our cherished recipes—the mainstay of our seasonal repasts at the river's side.

SPRING

WHEN SPRING IS
IN THE AIR

Spring lifted winter's blanket and robed the city in a floral array. Brilliant azalea colors, combined with the soft hues of tulip magnolias and flowering pear trees, brought New Bern's gardens and surrounding landscapes to life. Residents returned to the out-of-doors to plant their vegetable gardens and entertain their neighbors. The porch or the verandah once again became the center of the universe, and conversations flowed more freely on a lazy Saturday afternoon. During the Victorian era, chicken salad and a buttery pound cake were just a few of the delectable treats New Bernians might have served as the afternoon's repast.

SYMPHONIES, SPRING HOMES
AND ALL THAT JAZZ
PAGE 13

SUPPER CLUB
PAGE 26

HOLE IN ONE
PAGE 44

COLDWELL BANKER

WILLIS-SMITH
COMPANY

Supper Club

Symphonies, Spring Homes and all that Jazz

Beverage
Strawberry Smoothie

Appetizers
Quick and Easy Pinwheels

Bacon-Cheese Fingers • Chicken Salad Tartlets

Spinach Bacon Dip

Soup
Shrimp Chippewa Soup

Main Dishes
Breakfast Casserole

Crab Quiche

Side Dishes
Pineapple Casserole

Hash Brown Potato Casserole

Michelle's Spinach Pie

Breads
Nutty Banana Bread • Hatteras Baked Pancake

Desserts
Chocolate Almond Cake

Lemon Squares

Guilt-Free Cheesecake

Strawberry Smoothie

    1   frozen banana, sliced
    1   cup vanilla nonfat yogurt
    1   (10-ounce) package frozen sliced strawberries
    1/4 cup orange juice
    1   tablespoon honey

Combine the banana, yogurt, strawberries, orange juice and honey in a blender container. Process until smooth, scraping down the sides once. Serve immediately.

Yield: 3 servings

Quick and Easy Pinwheels

    1   (3-ounce) package dried beef, or 2 (5-ounce) cans chunk ham
    16   ounces cream cheese, softened
    1   envelope ranch salad dressing mix
    4   or 5 green onion tops, chopped
    1   (4-ounce) can chopped black olives, drained (optional)
    1/2 cup chopped jalapeño chiles, or to taste (optional)
    10   large flour tortillas

Chop the dried beef. Combine the dried beef, cream cheese, salad dressing mix, green onions, olives and jalapeño chiles in a bowl and mix well.

Spread the cream cheese mixture in a thin layer over each tortilla. Roll the tortillas to enclose the filling and place, seam side down, on a platter.

Chill, covered, for 2 to 3 hours. Cut into slices and place on a serving platter.

Note: You may substitute green chiles for the jalapeño chiles, turkey for the beef, and/or low-fat cream cheese for the cream cheese.

Yield: 60 appetizers

BACON-CHEESE FINGERS

10 slices dried bread, trimmed
1   cup shredded Swiss cheese
8   slices bacon, crisp-cooked, crumbled
3   to 4 tablespoons mayonnaise
1   tablespoon grated onion
1/2 teaspoon celery salt

Cut each slice of bread into thirds. Combine the cheese, bacon, mayonnaise, onion and celery salt in a bowl and mix well. Spread over each piece of bread. Place the bread fingers on a baking sheet. Bake at 325 degrees for 10 minutes.

Yield: 30 appetizers

CHICKEN SALAD TARTLETS

4   to 6 chicken breast halves
3   hard-cooked eggs
1   (8-ounce) jar sandwich spread
1   (8-ounce) jar mayonnaise
1/2 cup salad cubes
1 1/2 cups chopped celery
    Salt and pepper to taste
36 baked tartlet shells

Bring enough water to cover the chicken breasts to a boil in a saucepan. Add the chicken. Cook until tender and cooked through; drain. Let stand until cool. Chop the chicken finely, discarding the skin and bones.

Chop the eggs finely. Combine the chicken, eggs, sandwich spread, mayonnaise, salad cubes and celery in a bowl and mix well. Season with salt and pepper. Spoon the chicken mixture into the tartlet shells. Chill, covered, until ready to serve.

Yield: 36 appetizers

SPINACH BACON DIP

1   (10-ounce) package frozen chopped spinach, thawed
3   ounces bacon bits
1   envelope ranch salad dressing mix
1   cup mayonnaise or fat-free mayonnaise
1   cup sour cream
1   bunch green onions, finely chopped

Drain the spinach, pressing out the excess moisture. Combine the spinach, bacon bits, salad dressing mix, mayonnaise, sour cream and green onions in a bowl and mix well.

Chill, covered, for 2 hours. Spoon into a serving bowl.

Yield: 3 cups

SHRIMP CHIPPEWA SOUP

$1/2$ cup (1 stick) butter
$2^1/2$ pounds peeled shrimp
$1^1/2$ cups sliced mushrooms
4   garlic cloves, minced
7   cups chicken broth, boiling
$1^1/2$ cups chopped green onions
$1/2$ cup chopped parsley
$1/2$ cup (1 stick) butter

Heat $1/2$ cup butter in a large saucepan until melted. Add the shrimp, mushrooms and garlic. Sauté until the shrimp turn pink.

Stir the chicken broth, green onions and parsley into the shrimp mixture. Remove from the heat. Add $1/2$ cup butter, stirring until melted.

Ladle into soup bowls. Serve with French bread.

Yield: 6 to 8 servings

BREAKFAST CASSEROLE

    Butter
6   slices bread, trimmed
1   pound bulk pork sausage
2   cups half-and-half
6   eggs, beaten
1   teaspoon salt
5   ounces Cheddar cheese, shredded

Butter both sides of the bread. Cut the bread into cubes. Sprinkle over the bottom of a 3-quart baking dish.

Brown the sausage in a skillet, stirring until crumbly; drain. Spoon over the bread.

Combine the half-and-half, eggs and salt in a bowl and mix well. Pour over the sausage. Chill, covered, for 8 to 12 hours.

Bake at 400 degrees for 45 to 55 minutes or until set, checking after 30 minutes. Sprinkle the cheese over the top. Bake until cheese is melted.

Yield: 10 to 12 servings

Variation

BREAKFAST PIZZA

Substitute one 8-ounce can refrigerated crescent rolls for the bread and mozzarella cheese for the Cheddar cheese. Decrease the half-and-half to 1/2 cup. Unroll the dough. Separate into 8 triangles.

Place over the bottom of a greased 12-inch pizza pan, pressing the perforations to seal. Brown the sausage in a skillet, stirring until crumbly; drain. Sprinkle over the dough.

Combine the half-and-half, eggs and salt in a bowl and mix well. Pour over the sausage. Bake at 425 degrees for 15 minutes or until set. Sprinkle the cheese over the top. Bake until cheese is melted.

The New Bern Historical Society was begun in the early 1920s with a mission, "To preserve for future generations the wealth of historical material found here in New Bern." The restored Attmore-Oliver House, purchased in 1953, is the home of the New Bern Historical Society.

CRAB QUICHE

- 1/2 cup mayonnaise
- 2 tablespoons flour
- 2 eggs, beaten
- 1/2 cup milk
- 1 (6-ounce) can imitation crab meat, drained
- 8 ounces Swiss cheese, cut into 1/4-inch cubes
- 1/2 cup chopped green onions
- 1 unbaked (9-inch) pie shell

Combine the mayonnaise, flour, eggs and milk in a bowl and mix well. Stir in the crab meat, cheese and green onions. Spoon into the pie shell.

Bake at 350 degrees for 30 to 40 minutes or until set.

Yield: 6 servings

PINEAPPLE CASSEROLE

- 1/4 cup (1/2 stick) margarine, melted
- 1 cup sugar
- 2 eggs
- 1 (20-ounce) can crushed pineapple
- 1 cup bread crumbs

Combine the margarine, sugar and eggs in a bowl and mix well. Stir in the pineapple and bread crumbs. Spoon into a greased baking dish. Bake at 350 degrees for 45 minutes.

Yield: 4 to 6 servings

HASH BROWN POTATO CASSEROLE

1   (32-ounce) bag frozen hash brown potatoes
1   cup sour cream
1/2   cup (1 stick) margarine, melted
1/2   cup chopped onion
1   (10-ounce) can cream of chicken soup
8   ounces mild Cheddar cheese, shredded
1 1/2 teaspoons salt

Combine the potatoes, sour cream, margarine, onion, soup, cheese and salt in a bowl and mix well. Spoon into a greased 9×13-inch baking dish.

Bake at 350 degrees for 1 hour and 15 minutes.

Note: You may freeze the casserole before baking. Bring the casserole to room temperature and bake as directed.

Yield: 10 to 12 servings

Today New Bernians continue the legacy begun by the likes of Mrs. Gertrude Carraway and others, opening their homes to visitors from as far away as California. New Bern's Spring Homes Tour heralds the advent of spring, a much-celebrated event in this historic town that bursts at the seams with flowering trees and gardens. Hostesses can rest their feet while eating the delectable treats served at a brunch or lunch following their "time on duty."

MICHELLE'S SPINACH PIE

1   (17-ounce) package puff pastry, thawed
2   (10-ounce) packages frozen chopped spinach
1   onion, chopped
1   or 2 eggs
8   ounces Swiss or Cheddar cheese, shredded
    Chopped parsley (optional)
    Dash of nutmeg
    Salt and pepper to taste

Roll one sheet of the puff pastry into a 12-inch circle on a lightly floured surface. Fit into a pie plate.

Cook the spinach using the package directions; drain thoroughly. Combine with the onion, eggs, cheese, parsley and nutmeg in a bowl and mix well. Season with salt and pepper.

Spoon into the pastry-lined pie plate. Top with the remaining puff pastry sheet, sealing the edge and cutting vents.

Bake at 400 degrees for 40 minutes or until golden brown.

Yield: 6 servings

NUTTY BANANA BREAD

1/2 cup butter-flavor shortening
1 cup sugar
2 eggs
2 cups self-rising flour
3 ripe bananas, mashed (about 1 cup)
1 cup chopped nuts

Cream the shortening and sugar in a mixing bowl until light and fluffy. Beat in the eggs. Add the flour and mix well. Add the bananas and mix well. Stir in the nuts.

Spoon into a greased loaf pan. Bake at 300 degrees for 1 hour.

Yield: 1 loaf

Saxophone and clarinet tunes fill the air, and picnic meals fill baskets, during the Beaufort Music Festival held each April in Beaufort "By the Sea," or during Tryon Palace's "Symphony on the Lawn," always held in mid-June.

$\mathcal{H}$ATTERAS BAKED PANCAKE

As distinctive as the boats bearing the Hatteras name, this pancake will add a touch of class to any special breakfast event. You will receive raves on this embarrassingly simple recipe.

Pancake

3   eggs
3/4 cup unbleached white flour
3/4 cup milk
1/2 teaspoon salt
1/2 teaspoon vanilla or lemon extract
1 1/2 tablespoons butter

Apple Topping

1/4 cup (1/2 stick) butter
4   Granny Smith apples, peeled, cut into slices
    Honey
    Brown sugar
    Dash of cinnamon
    Dash of nutmeg

For the pancake, beat the eggs, flour, milk, salt and vanilla in a mixing bowl until smooth.

Heat the butter in a cast-iron 12-inch skillet until melted, swirling to coat the bottom. Pour the batter into the skillet.

Bake in a preheated 450-degree oven for 15 minutes. Reduce the temperature to 350 degrees. Bake for an additional 10 minutes.

For the topping, heat the butter in a heavy skillet until melted. Add the apples. Sauté for 7 to 10 minutes or until tender. Drizzle with honey. Sprinkle with brown sugar, cinnamon and nutmeg. Cook until apples are heated through and tender.

Spoon the Apple Topping over the center of the pancake. Sprinkle with confectioners' sugar.

Yield: 4 to 6 servings

CHOCOLATE ALMOND CAKE

1 cup corn oil
1/2 cup (1 stick) margarine
1 cup water
1/4 cup baking cocoa
2 cups flour
1 tablespoon cinnamon
1 tablespoon vanilla extract
2 cups sugar
1/2 cup milk
1/2 teaspoon almond extract
2 eggs
Chocolate Almond Icing (at right)

Combine the corn oil, margarine, water and baking cocoa in a large saucepan. Bring to a boil, stirring frequently. Remove from the heat.

Add the flour, cinnamon, vanilla, sugar, milk and almond extract to the hot mixture and mix well. Add the eggs and mix well. Pour into a greased 9×13-inch cake pan.

Bake at 325 degrees for 25 minutes or until a wooden pick inserted in the center comes out clean. Cool in the pans for 10 minutes. Remove to a wire rack to cool completely.

Spread Chocolate Almond Icing between the layers and over the top and side of the cooled cake.

Yield: 15 servings

CHOCOLATE ALMOND ICING

1/2 cup (1 stick) margarine, softened
1 (1-pound) package confectioners' sugar
1/4 cup baking cocoa
1 tablespoon vanilla extract
1/2 teaspoon almond extract
Milk

Cream the margarine and confectioners' sugar in a mixing bowl until light and fluffy. Add the baking cocoa, vanilla and almond extract. Add enough milk to make of spreading consistency.

LEMON SQUARES

New Bern, which
gave the world its
first Pepsi-Cola at
Caleb Bradham's Drug
Store in 1899,
found itself once
again in the
mainstream of world
history in 1942 and
1943 as encroaching
German submarines
moved periously
close through
coastal waters.

2   cups flour
1/2 cup confectioners' sugar
1   cup (2 sticks) butter
1/4 cup flour
1/2 teaspoon baking powder
4   eggs
2   cups sugar
1/3 cup lemon juice
     Confectioners' sugar

Sift 2 cups flour and 1/2 cup confectioners' sugar together in a bowl. Cut in the butter until crumbly. Press over the bottom of a 9×13-inch baking pan. Bake at 350 degrees for 15 to 20 minutes or until light brown.

Sift 1/4 cup flour and baking powder together. Beat the eggs, sugar and lemon juice together in a mixing bowl. Add the sifted flour mixture and mix well. Pour over the baked crust.

Bake at 350 degrees for 20 to 25 minutes or until set. Sprinkle with confectioners' sugar. Run a knife around the edges to loosen. Cool on a wire rack. Cut into squares.

Yield: 35 squares

$\mathcal{G}$UILT-FREE CHEESECAKE

1/3 cup graham cracker crumbs
24 ounces fat-free cream cheese, softened
3/4 cup sugar
1 teaspoon vanilla extract
3 eggs
1 1/2 cups sliced strawberries

Spray a 9-inch pie plate with nonstick cooking spray. Sprinkle the graham cracker crumbs over the bottom.

Combine the cream cheese, sugar and vanilla in a mixing bowl. Beat at medium speed until blended. Add the eggs. Beat just until blended; do not overbeat. Pour into the prepared pie plate.

Bake at 325 degrees for 45 minutes or until center is almost set. Let stand until cooled. Chill, covered, for 3 hours or longer. Arrange the strawberry slices over the top before serving.

Yield: 10 servings

Supper Club

Appetizers
Stuffed Mushrooms • Nancy's Chipped Beef
Supper Club Pepper Pesto and Paprika Chips

Soups
Chicken, Beans and Greens Soup
Speedy Black Bean Soup

Salads
Caesar Salad with Portobello Mushrooms
Green Salad with Asparagus, Orange and Red Onion

Main Dishes
Mostaccioli

Chicken and Artichokes

Margaret Dolan's Crab Meat Imperial

Low Country Shrimp and Grits • Low Country Jambalaya

Side Dishes
Broccoli Supreme
Curried Rice

Breads
Easy Italian Bread
Grandpa's Homemade Bread

Desserts
Chocolate Lover's Cake with Chocolate Buttercream Frosting
Ginger Cointreau Sherbet
Meringues Chantilly

Stuffed Mushrooms

24   ounces mushrooms
1   pound bulk pork sausage
8   ounces cream cheese
1   cup herb-seasoned stuffing mix

Wash the mushrooms and pat them dry. Remove and discard the stems; set aside the caps. Brown the sausage in a skillet, stirring until crumbly; drain. Add the cream cheese and stuffing mix and mix well. Stuff the mushroom caps with the sausage mixture. Place the stuffed caps on a baking sheet. Bake at 350 degrees for 15 to 30 minutes or until heated through.

Yield: about 36 mushrooms

Nancy's Chipped Beef

16   ounces cream cheese, softened
1/4 cup milk
2   (5-ounce) jars chipped beef, finely chopped
1/2 cup finely chopped green bell pepper
1/4 cup instant minced onions
1   teaspoon garlic salt
1/2 teaspoon pepper
1   cup sour cream
1/4 cup (1/2 stick) butter
1   cup chopped pecans
1   teaspoon salt

Combine the cream cheese and milk in a bowl and mix well. Stir in the chipped beef, bell pepper, onions, garlic salt and pepper. Fold in the sour cream. Spoon into a 1-quart baking dish, spreading evenly. Melt the butter in a skillet. Add the pecans and salt. Cook until the pecans are crisp and toasted, stirring constantly. Sprinkle the pecans over the top. Bake at 350 degrees for 20 minutes.

Yield: about 32 (2-tablespoon) servings

Long known for their entertaining flair, New Bernians love to host their good friends in their homes in casual, but elegant, style. Supper Club makes this an easy way to have a dinner party, with each couple assigned to bring either the appetizer, dessert, salad, or side dish. Several Supper Clubs are long-standing traditions, having been in existence for ten years or more. Christ Episcopal Church expanded this to include travel, thus the METS—Meet, Eat and Travel Society.

SUPPER CLUB PEPPER PESTO

PAPRIKA CHIPS

1/2 teaspoon each hot
    or sweet paprika,
    ground fennel
    seeds and onion
    powder
1/4 teaspoon salt
1/4 teaspoon cinnamon
4   pita breads
1/4 cup vegetable oil

Combine the first
5 ingredients in a small
bowl and mix well.
Split each pita bread in
half. Brush the rough
sides of the pita rounds
with oil. Sprinkle with
the paprika mixture.

Stack the rounds and
cut into 64 wedges.
Arrange the wedges,
seasoned sides up on
2 baking sheets. Bake
at 350 degrees for 9
minutes or until crisp
and lightly browned.

1   (12-ounce) jar roasted red peppers, drained
1/2 cup fresh cilantro leaves
1   tablespoon tomato paste
1   tablespoon sherry vinegar
2   teaspoons fresh lemon juice
1 1/2 teaspoons minced garlic
1 1/4 teaspoons kosher salt
1/2 teaspoon hot or sweet paprika
1/2 teaspoon chili powder
1/4 teaspoon cayenne pepper
1   cup coarsely ground blanched almonds
    Paprika Chips (at left)

Place the roasted peppers, cilantro, tomato paste, vinegar, lemon juice, garlic, salt, paprika, chili powder and cayenne pepper in a blender or food processor container. Pulse until the peppers and cilantro are finely chopped. Scrape down the side of the container. Process until the mixture is smooth. Add the almonds and pulse until combined. Serve with Paprika Chips.

Note: The pesto may be prepared up to 2 days ahead of time, covered and refrigerated.

Yield: 16 (2-tablespoon) servings

CHICKEN, BEANS AND GREENS SOUP

1/3 cup olive oil
2 garlic cloves, minced
1/2 cup coarsely chopped carrots
1/2 cup coarsely chopped celery
1/2 cup coarsely chopped onion or leek
1 pound boneless skinless chicken breast halves,
cut into 1/2-inch chunks
8 cups chicken broth
1 (14-ounce) can Italian-style stewed tomatoes
1 cup uncooked ditalini or other small pasta
4 cups loosely packed chopped kale or escarole
1 (19-ounce) can cannellini or white kidney beans
1/4 teaspoon salt
1/4 teaspoon freshly ground pepper
Grated Parmesan cheese

Heat the olive oil in a large heavy pot over medium heat. Add the garlic and sauté for 1 minute or until fragrant. Stir in the carrots, celery and onion. Cook for 3 to 4 minutes or until almost tender. Add the chicken. Cook for 3 minutes or until the chicken turns opaque, stirring frequently.

Stir in the broth and tomatoes. Cover and bring to a boil over high heat. Add the ditalini. Reduce the heat to low. Simmer, uncovered, for 10 minutes or until the pasta is almost tender, stirring occasionally. Stir in the kale. Simmer, uncovered, for 20 minutes or until the kale is very tender. Add the cannellini, salt and pepper. Simmer for 5 minutes.

Ladle the soup into bowls. Sprinkle each serving with Parmesan cheese.

Yield: 8 servings

SPEEDY BLACK BEAN SOUP

1   teaspoon olive oil

3/4 cup chopped onion

2   (15-ounce) cans black beans

1   (14-ounce) can fat-free chicken broth

1   (15-ounce) can whole kernel corn, drained

1   (14-ounce) can Mexican-style stewed tomatoes

3   bay leaves

1   teaspoon minced garlic

1   teaspoon thyme

1   teaspoon balsamic vinegar

1/2 teaspoon cumin

Heat the olive oil in a 4-quart Dutch oven over medium heat. Add the onion. Cook until slightly browned, stirring occasionally.

Pour 1 can of the black beans into a medium bowl. Mash the beans against the side of the bowl with a large metal spoon until broken up and of a paste consistency. Add the mashed beans, broth and the remaining can of whole black beans to the onion and mix well. Stir in the corn, tomatoes, bay leaves, garlic, thyme, vinegar and cumin.

Cover and bring to a boil over high heat. Reduce the heat to low. Simmer for 8 minutes, stirring frequently to prevent sticking. Remove from the heat. Remove and discard the bay leaves and serve immediately.

Yield: 6 servings

CAESAR SALAD WITH PORTOBELLO MUSHROOMS

9   anchovies, minced
3   tablespoons fresh lemon juice
1 1/2 tablespoons Dijon mustard
2   garlic cloves, minced
1/2 cup olive oil
1   medium head romaine, cut into bite-size pieces
1   large head radicchio, cut into bite-size pieces
3   large portobello mushrooms (3/4 pound)
3   tablespoons olive oil
4   garlic cloves, peeled and flattened
     Salt and pepper to taste
1/4 cup chopped fresh parsley
1 1/3 cups grated Parmesan cheese

Combine the anchovies, lemon juice, mustard and 2 cloves minced garlic in a small bowl. Whisk in 1/2 cup olive oil gradually. Set the dressing aside.

Toss the romaine and radicchio in a large bowl; set aside.

Remove and discard the stems from the mushrooms. Slice the mushroom caps crosswise into 3/8-inch-thick strips.

Heat 3 tablespoons olive oil in a large heavy skillet over medium heat. Add 4 cloves flattened garlic. Cook for 4 minutes; remove and discard the garlic. Increase the heat to medium-high. Sauté the mushrooms in the skillet for 4 minutes on each side or until browned. Remove from the heat. Season with salt and pepper. Sprinkle with the parsley.

Stir the dressing, pour over the salad greens and toss to coat. Stir in the Parmesan cheese and season with salt and pepper. Divide the salad among 6 plates. Top with the mushrooms and serve immediately.

Yield: 6 servings

GREEN SALAD WITH ASPARAGUS, ORANGE AND RED ONION

Buttermilk Dressing

- 2/3 cup regular or low-fat mayonnaise
- 1/2 cup buttermilk
- 3 tablespoons each olive oil and white wine vinegar
- 3 tablespoons chopped fresh basil, or 1 tablespoon dried basil
- 2 tablespoons chopped fresh tarragon, or 2 teaspoons dried tarragon

Salad

- 24 fresh asparagus spears, trimmed
- 4 oranges
- 12 cups mixed baby salad greens
- 1 tablespoon chopped fresh basil, or 1 teaspoon dried basil
- 1 tablespoon chopped fresh tarragon, or 1 teaspoon dried tarragon
- 1/2 cup thinly sliced red onion, separated into rings

For the dressing, whisk the mayonnaise, buttermilk, olive oil, vinegar, basil and tarragon in a medium bowl until well blended. Chill until cold.

For the salad, bring a large pot of water to a boil. Add the asparagus. Cook for 2 minutes or until tender-crisp. Remove the asparagus to a bowl of ice water; let stand until cool. Drain and set aside.

Peel the oranges with a sharp paring knife, removing the white pith and membrane. Make 2 cuts on each side of each orange section to completely release it from the membrane.

Arrange the asparagus spears in a sunburst pattern on a serving platter. Place the orange sections between the asparagus spears. Mound the greens in the center of the platter and sprinkle with the basil and tarragon. Top with the red onion slices. Drizzle some of the dressing over the salad. Pour the remaining dressing into a bottle to serve separately.

Yield: 8 servings

MOSTACCIOLI

1 pound beef summer sausage, cut into bite-size pieces
1/2 cup chopped onion
1/4 cup chopped green bell pepper
2 (8-ounce) cans tomato sauce
1 (14-ounce) can diced tomatoes
1 garlic clove, minced
1/2 teaspoon salt
1/4 teaspoon oregano
1/8 teaspoon pepper
16 ounces mostaccioli or rigatoni, cooked, drained
1 to 2 cups shredded mozzarella cheese

Combine the sausage, onion, bell pepper, tomato sauce and diced tomatoes in a large saucepan. Stir in the garlic, salt, oregano and pepper. Cook over medium heat for 10 minutes.

Add the mostaccioli to the sauce mixture and mix well. Spoon into a 3-quart baking dish. Top with the mozzarella cheese.

Bake at 350 degrees for 20 to 25 minutes. Serve with salad and garlic bread.

Yield: 8 servings

CHICKEN AND ARTICHOKES

1 cup sliced fresh mushrooms
1/4 cup finely chopped onion
1 garlic clove, minced
12 tablespoons (1 1/2 sticks) butter
4 boneless skinless chicken breast halves, cut into strips
1/4 cup dry white wine
1/4 cup flour
1 1/2 cups milk
    Salt and pepper to taste
2 (14-ounce) cans artichoke hearts, drained, chopped
1/4 cup grated Parmesan cheese
1 teaspoon chopped fresh parsley

Cook the mushrooms, onion and garlic in 3 tablespoons of the butter in a skillet over medium-low heat. Remove from the skillet and set aside.

Melt 5 tablespoons of the butter in the same skillet over medium heat. Add the chicken strips. Cook for 10 minutes or until the chicken is tender, stirring constantly. Stir in the wine. Cook for 5 minutes. Add the mushroom mixture and mix well.

Melt the remaining 4 tablespoons butter in a small skillet. Whisk in the flour until blended and smooth, stirring constantly. Whisk in the milk gradually. Cook until the mixture thickens, whisking constantly. Season with salt and pepper. Stir in the artichokes and Parmesan cheese.

Spoon the chicken mixture into a 7×11-inch baking dish. Top evenly with the artichoke sauce. Bake at 300 degrees for 15 minutes or until bubbly. Sprinkle the parsley over the top and serve hot.

Yield: 4 servings

MARGARET DOLAN'S CRAB MEAT IMPERIAL

1/4 cup light cream
3   tablespoons butter, melted
2   tablespoons mayonnaise
2   tablespoons chopped green bell pepper
2   tablespoons chopped fresh parsley
1 1/2 tablespoons finely chopped onion
1   tablespoon prepared yellow mustard
1   teaspoon lemon juice
1   teaspoon dry mustard
1/4 teaspoon salt
1/4 teaspoon cayenne pepper
1/4 teaspoon celery seeds
1   pound crab meat

Combine the cream, butter, mayonnaise, bell pepper, parsley, onion, prepared mustard, lemon juice, dry mustard, salt, cayenne pepper and celery seeds in a medium bowl. Add the crab meat and stir lightly to prevent the crab from breaking up.

Spoon the crab mixture into a greased 8×8-inch baking dish. Bake at 350 degrees for 20 to 30 minutes or until bubbly.

Note: You may substitute 3 tablespoons mayonnaise and 1/4 cup milk for the 2 tablespoons mayonnaise and 1/4 cup light cream.

Yield: 4 servings

Oriental, the "Sailing Capital of North Carolina," is located approximately 28 miles from New Bern on the northern banks of the Neuse River. A ten-foot channel connects Oriental with the Intracoastal Waterway. Oriental is also known for its crab meat, which is distinguished by its unique sweet, firm white lump meat. Jumbo Lump is the highest grade of crab meat available. Carolina crab meat is a blend selected from the male crab for the large lumps, and the female for its sweetness.

$\mathcal{L}$OW COUNTRY SHRIMP AND GRITS

1 1/2 cups milk
1   cup light cream or half-and-half
1   cup water
1   cup (2 sticks) butter
      Pinch of baking soda
1   cup stone-ground grits
2   pounds peeled cooked shrimp
      Juice of 1 lemon
1   teaspoon Worcestershire sauce

Heat the milk, cream, water, 1/2 cup of the butter and the baking soda in a saucepan over medium-low heat until boiling. Stir in the grits slowly. Cook for 20 minutes, stirring frequently. Cover and place over simmering water. Cook for 30 minutes.

Melt the remaining 1/2 cup butter in a large skillet. Add the shrimp and cook just until heated through; do not overcook. Stir in the lemon juice and Worcestershire sauce. Serve the shrimp mixture over the hot grits.

Yield: 6 servings

$\mathcal{L}$OW COUNTRY JAMBALAYA

8 ounces bacon, cut into 1/2-inch strips
1 large onion, minced
2 green bell peppers, chopped
1 cup uncooked rice
1 (16-ounce) can stewed tomatoes, chopped
1 3/4 cups (or more) regular or low-sodium chicken broth
14 to 16 ounces turkey kielbasa, sliced
2 to 3 grilled boneless chicken breast halves, cut into strips
2 to 3 teaspoons Cajun seasoning
1 tablespoon chopped fresh basil, or 1 teaspoon dried basil
1 teaspoon minced garlic
1 teaspoon salt
   Pepper to taste
1 pound fresh deveined peeled medium shrimp

Sauté the bacon in a large skillet until browned but not crisp. Remove the bacon with a slotted spoon and set aside.

Add the onion to the bacon drippings in the skillet. Sauté until transparent. Add the bell peppers. Cook for 3 to 4 minutes. Stir in the rice. Cook until the rice turns opaque and is thoroughly coated with drippings. Add the bacon, tomatoes, broth, kielbasa, chicken, Cajun seasoning, basil, garlic, salt and pepper and mix well. Bring to a boil. Reduce the heat to low. Cook for 2 minutes.

Pour the jambalaya mixture into an ovenproof Dutch oven or 4-quart baking dish. Bake at 350 degrees for 35 to 40 minutes, adding more broth or water as needed. Stir in the shrimp, pushing them down into the rice. Bake for 10 minutes longer. Serve immediately.

Yield: 6 to 8 servings

BROCCOLI SUPREME

1   (18-ounce) can cream-style corn
1   (10- to 16-ounce) package frozen chopped broccoli, thawed
1   egg, lightly beaten
1   tablespoon grated onion
1/4 teaspoon salt
     Dash of pepper
3   tablespoons butter or margarine, melted
1   cup herb-seasoned stuffing mix

Combine the corn, broccoli, egg, onion, salt and pepper in a bowl and mix well. Combine the butter and stuffing mix in a small bowl, tossing to coat. Stir 3/4 cup of the stuffing mixture into the vegetable mixture. Spoon into a 1-quart baking dish. Sprinkle with the remaining stuffing mixture. Bake at 350 degrees for 35 to 40 minutes.

Yield: 4 to 6 servings

CURRIED RICE

3   tablespoons butter
1/2 cup finely chopped onion
1   garlic clove, minced
1   apple, peeled, diced
1   tablespoon curry powder
1   cup converted rice
1 1/2 cups chicken broth
1   bay leaf

Melt 2 tablespoons of the butter in a heavy saucepan. Add the onion and garlic. Cook until the onion is tender. Stir in the apple, curry powder, rice, broth and bay leaf. Bring to a boil. Reduce the heat to low. Simmer, covered, for 17 minutes. Remove from the heat and discard the bay leaf. Add the remaining 1 tablespoon butter and fluff the rice with a fork.

Yield: 4 servings

$\mathcal{E}$ASY ITALIAN BREAD

2   cups flour
2   envelopes dry yeast
1   tablespoon sugar
2   teaspoons salt
1³/4 cups water
1   tablespoon butter
2¹/2 cups flour
    Cornmeal
2   egg whites, lightly beaten
    Dash of garlic powder

Combine 2 cups flour, yeast, sugar and salt in a large mixing bowl and mix well.

Heat the water and butter to 130 degrees in a saucepan. Add to the flour mixture. Beat for 2 minutes. Stir in 2¹/2 cups flour to make a soft dough.

Knead the dough on a floured surface for 10 minutes or until smooth and elastic. Cover and let rest for 20 minutes.

Divide the dough into halves. Shape each half into a ball. Roll out each ball into a long rectangle on a lightly floured surface. Roll as for a jelly roll to form a loaf. Place the loaves seam side down on a greased baking sheet sprinkled with cornmeal. Let rise, covered, in a warm place for 1 hour or until doubled in bulk.

Bake at 400 degrees for 20 minutes. Combine the egg whites and garlic powder in a small bowl. Brush over the tops of the loaves. Bake for 5 minutes. Remove from the baking sheet. Cool on a wire rack.

Note: This dough also makes a good pizza crust.

Yield: 20 servings

GRANDPA'S HOMEMADE BREAD

2   cups milk
2   cups water
1/4   cup light corn syrup or honey
2   tablespoons shortening
4   teaspoons salt
1   cake yeast
1/4   cup warm water (105 to 115 degrees)
12   cups (about) flour

Scald the milk in a saucepan. Pour the hot milk into a large heatproof bowl. Add 2 cups water, corn syrup, shortening and salt. Cool the mixture to lukewarm.

Soften the yeast in 1/4 cup warm water in a small bowl. Stir the yeast mixture into the warm milk mixture. Add enough flour to make a stiff dough.

Knead the dough on a floured surface until smooth and elastic. Shape the dough into a ball and place in a greased bowl, turning to coat the surface. Let rise, covered, in a warm place for 4 to 5 hours or until doubled in bulk. Punch the dough down. Let rise again until doubled in bulk.

Punch the dough down. Divide it into 4 equal portions. Shape each portion into a ball. Cover and let rest for 10 to 15 minutes.

Shape into 4 loaves and place in 4 greased loaf pans. Let rise until doubled in bulk. Bake at 400 degrees for 40 to 45 minutes. Remove from the pans. Cool on wire racks.

Yield: 48 servings (4 loaves)

CHOCOLATE LOVER'S CAKE

2   ounces unsweetened chocolate
1/4   cup sugar
3   tablespoons water
3/4   cup (1 1/2 sticks) butter, softened
2   cups sugar
4   egg yolks
1   teaspoon vanilla extract
2 1/4   cups sifted cake flour
1   teaspoon cream of tartar
1/2   teaspoon baking soda
1/2   teaspoon salt
1   cup milk
4   egg whites, stiffly beaten
    Chocolate Buttercream Frosting (at right)

Line three greased 9-inch round cake pans with waxed paper.

Melt the chocolate in a small saucepan. Stir in 1/4 cup sugar and water; set aside.

Cream the butter and 2 cups sugar in a mixing bowl until light and fluffy. Beat in the egg yolks 1 at a time. Add the chocolate mixture and vanilla and mix well.

Sift the flour, cream of tartar, baking soda and salt together. Add the sifted dry ingredients and milk alternately to the creamed mixture, mixing well after each addition. Fold in the stiffly beaten egg whites. Pour into the prepared pans.

Bake at 350 degrees for 18 to 20 minutes or until the layers test done. Cool in the pans for 10 minutes. Remove to wire racks to cool completely. Spread the Chocolate Buttercream Frosting between the layers and over the top and side of the cooled cake.

Yield: 12 servings

CHOCOLATE BUTTERCREAM FROSTING

1/2   cup (1 stick) butter, softened
4   ounces cream cheese, softened
1   (1-pound) package confectioners' sugar, sifted
3 1/2   ounces German's sweet chocolate, melted
1   tablespoon vanilla extract
2   to 3 tablespoons milk

Cream the butter, cream cheese and confectioners' sugar in a mixing bowl until light and fluffy. Add the melted chocolate, vanilla and enough milk to make of a spreading consistency.

GINGER COINTREAU SHERBET

1 1/2 cups water
3/4 cup sugar
1 cup orange juice
1/2 cup lemon juice
1/2 cup Cointreau
3 (10-ounce) bottles ginger ale

Combine the water and sugar in a saucepan. Bring to a boil, stirring until the sugar is completely dissolved. Reduce the heat to low. Simmer for 5 minutes. Remove from the heat and cool.

Stir in the orange juice, lemon juice, Cointreau and ginger ale and mix well. Pour into a freezer container and freeze until firm.

Yield: 8 servings

MERINGUES CHANTILLY

4 egg whites, at room temperature
2/3 cup superfine sugar
2/3 cup confectioners' sugar
2 cups whipping cream, chilled
2 tablespoons superfine sugar

Beat the egg whites in a large mixing bowl until soft peaks form. Add 1/3 cup of the superfine sugar gradually, beating until stiff peaks form and the meringue is smooth and shiny. Add the remaining 1/3 cup of the superfine sugar. Beat for 2 minutes at low speed. Fold in the confectioners' sugar gently with a rubber spatula.

Spoon the meringue into a pastry bag fitted with a 3/4-inch fluted tip. Pipe the meringue onto a buttered and floured baking sheet into small domes or swirls.

Bake the meringues at 225 degrees for about 1 hour or until ivory colored but not brown. (If the meringues begin to brown too quickly, reduce the oven temperature.) Remove the baked meringues with a metal spatula to wire racks to cool.

Shortly before serving, prepare the chantilly cream. Whip the cream in a mixing bowl until it begins to thicken. Add 2 tablespoons superfine sugar, beating until soft peaks form. Spoon the cream into a pastry bag fitted with a small round or fluted tip. Pipe the cream onto the flat sides of half the meringues. Top each with a plain meringue, flat sides together, to form sandwiches. Serve immediately.

Yield: 16 servings

Hole In One

Appetizers
Chicken Wraps
Hot Artichoke Dip
Onion Bread Spread

Soups
Black Dog Chicken Chili
Egg Drop Soup

Salads
Spring Pea Salad
Eighteen-Hole Salad

Main Dishes
Grilled Beef Tenderloin Tips
Sweet-and-Sour Meatballs
Golden Catfish Fillets
Cody's Seafood Gumbo "Louisiana Style"

Side Dishes
Black-eyed Pea Hoppin' John
Tangy Marinated Carrots
Corn Pudding
Rosemary Potatoes
Muriel Gray's Squash Casserole

Desserts
To-Die-For Chocolate Pecan Pie
Trophy Cookies
Hole-In-One Peanut Butter Cookies

CHICKEN WRAPS

3   large boneless skinless chicken breast halves
1   tablespoon peanut oil
1   small head cabbage, thinly sliced
1   large onion, thinly sliced
2   tablespoons peanut oil
8   ounces pimento cheese
8   ounces shredded Cheddar cheese
    Salt and pepper to taste
1   (16-ounce) package egg roll wrappers
4   cups peanut oil for deep-frying

Brown the chicken breasts in 1 tablespoon peanut oil in a skillet over medium-high heat until cooked through. Remove from the skillet. Cool slightly and cut into thin strips.

Sauté the cabbage and onion in 2 tablespoons peanut oil in the same skillet.

Combine the chicken strips, cabbage mixture, pimento cheese and Cheddar cheese in a bowl and mix well. Season with salt and pepper. Place 1/4 cup of the chicken mixture across a corner of each egg roll wrapper. Brush the edges of the wrapper with water. Roll to enclose the filling, folding in the corners.

Heat 4 cups peanut oil in a wok or large heavy saucepan to 375 degrees. Fry the rolls, a few at time, for 2 minutes or until golden brown. Drain on paper towels.

Yield: about 20 servings

Hot Artichoke Dip

1   (15-ounce) can artichoke hearts, drained, chopped
1   (4-ounce) jar marinated artichoke hearts, drained, chopped
1   cup mayonnaise
1   cup grated Parmesan cheese
1/2   cup chopped green onions
1   teaspoon garlic powder
1/2   teaspoon pepper
    Paprika

Combine the artichokes, mayonnaise, Parmesan cheese, green onions, garlic powder and pepper in a bowl and mix well. Spoon into a 1-quart baking dish, spreading evenly. Sprinkle with paprika.

Bake at 350 degrees for 20 minutes. Serve hot with crackers.

Yield: 28 (2-tablespoon) servings

Onion Bread Spread

1   cup chopped Vidalia onion
1   cup mayonnaise
1   cup shredded Swiss cheese
    French bread slices

Combine the onion, mayonnaise and cheese in a bowl and mix well. Spoon into a 9-inch pie plate, spreading evenly.

Bake at 350 degrees for 15 to 20 minutes or until bubbly. Spread over French bread slices to serve.

Note: You may use reduced-fat mayonnaise and cheese.

Yield: 24 (2-tablespoon) servings

BLACK DOG CHICKEN CHILI

2   pounds boneless skinless chicken breast halves,
     cut into 1/2-inch pieces
2   tablespoons vegetable oil
1   medium onion, chopped
4   garlic cloves, chopped
2   cups dried pinto beans, cooked, drained, or 3 (15-ounce) cans
     pinto beans, rinsed, drained
1   (14-ounce) can stewed tomatoes
1   cup chicken stock
1   (6-ounce) can chopped green chiles, drained
1/4 cup sun-dried tomatoes, chopped, or 2 to 3 tablespoons
     sun-dried tomato paste
1/2 bunch fresh cilantro, chopped
2   tablespoons chili powder
1   tablespoon cumin
1   teaspoon salt
1/2 teaspoon black pepper
1/2 teaspoon oregano
1/4 teaspoon cayenne pepper
     Shredded Cheddar cheese

Sauté the chicken in the oil in a Dutch oven for 5 minutes. Add the onion and garlic. Cook until the chicken is lightly browned.

Stir in the beans, stewed tomatoes, stock, chiles, sun-dried tomatoes, cilantro, chili powder, cumin, salt, black pepper, oregano and cayenne pepper. Bring to a boil. Reduce the heat to low. Simmer for 30 minutes. Serve topped with cheese and additional chopped cilantro.

Note: You may also add frozen corn, black beans and additional stewed tomatoes.

Yield: 6 servings

EGG DROP SOUP

Come spring, New Bernians are either in their boats or on the greens. New Bern boasts year-round golf at four golfing communities. Thoughts of Cody's Seafood Gumbo "Louisiana Style" (page 53) will hurry you off that tee box and over to the 19th Hole Celebration frequently held after rounds of golf at the various clubs around New Bern.

2	tablespoons cornstarch
1/4	cup cold water
4	cups chicken broth
1	scallion, minced (optional)
1	teaspoon sugar
1	teaspoon soy sauce
1	egg, lightly beaten
1	tablespoon cold water

Combine the cornstarch and 1/4 cup water in a small bowl and mix well; set aside.

Heat the broth and scallion in a heavy saucepan over medium heat to boiling. Stir in the sugar, soy sauce and cornstarch mixture. Heat until slightly thickened, stirring constantly.

Combine the egg and 1 tablespoon water in a measuring cup and mix well. Bring the soup to a full rolling boil. Remove from the heat. Drizzle in the egg mixture, stirring constantly.

Yield: 4 servings

SPRING PEA SALAD

      Lettuce leaves
1   *(15-ounce) can tiny peas, drained,*
      or 1 (15-ounce) bag frozen green peas, thawed
1/2 *cup each chopped onion and chopped celery*
3   *tablespoons mayonnaise*
6   *tablespoons grated Parmesan cheese*
3   *tablespoons sugar*

Line the bottom of a 1¹/₂-quart salad bowl with lettuce leaves. Layer the peas, onion and celery over the lettuce. Spread with the mayonnaise, sealing to the edge. Combine the Parmesan cheese and sugar in a bowl. Sprinkle over the mayonnaise. Chill, covered, in the refrigerator for 8 to 12 hours.

Yield: 6 to 8 servings

EIGHTEEN-HOLE SALAD

1   *head lettuce, chopped*
4   *hard-cooked eggs, sliced*
8   *ounces bacon, crisp-cooked, crumbled*
1   *(10-ounce) package frozen peas, thawed, drained*
1   *cup shredded Cheddar cheese*
1   *cup garlic ranch salad dressing*
1/2 *cup chopped green onions*

Place half the lettuce in a clear glass salad bowl with straight sides. Arrange the egg slices around the side of the bowl. Layer with the remaining lettuce, bacon, peas and cheese.

Spread the salad dressing over the cheese, sealing to the edge. Sprinkle with the green onions. Chill, covered, in the refrigerator for 8 to 12 hours.

Note: You may substitute mayonnaise for the ranch salad dressing and garnish top of salad with tomato wedges.

Yield: 6 servings

GRILLED BEEF TENDERLOIN TIPS

New Bern has a tradition of celebrating great events in the life of the town. In the 1850s all of New Bern came out and danced in the streets to welcome the extension of the railroad from Raleigh.

1/2 cup red wine
1/4 cup olive oil
1 tablespoon wine vinegar
1 tablespoon tarragon
1 teaspoon Worcestershire sauce
1 garlic clove, crushed
  Pepper to taste
2 pounds beef tenderloin tips, cut into 1-inch pieces
  Hot cooked rice

Combine the wine, olive oil, vinegar, tarragon, Worcestershire sauce, garlic and pepper in a bowl and mix well. Add the beef tips, stirring to coat. Marinate in the refrigerator for several hours.

Remove the beef from the marinade. Discard the marinade. Thread the beef onto skewers. Grill over medium coals until done to taste, turning frequently. Serve over rice.

Yield: 8 servings

SWEET-AND-SOUR MEATBALLS

1   pound lean ground beef
1/2   cup bread crumbs
1   egg, beaten
3   tablespoons A.1. steak sauce
1   garlic clove, crushed
1   teaspoon salt
1   tablespoon vegetable oil
1   (8-ounce) can pineapple chunks
1   cup sliced carrots
1   cup sliced celery
3/4   cup beef broth
2   tablespoons A.1. steak sauce
2   tablespoons soy sauce
1   tablespoon vinegar
1   teaspoon ginger
1   tablespoon cornstarch
1   tablespoon water
1   large green bell pepper, cut into strips
      Hot cooked rice

Combine the ground beef, bread crumbs, egg, 3 tablespoons steak sauce, garlic and salt in a bowl and mix well. Shape into 1-inch balls. Brown in oil on all sides in a large skillet; drain.

Stir in the pineapple, carrots, celery, broth, 2 tablespoons steak sauce, soy sauce, vinegar and ginger. Bring to a boil. Reduce the heat. Simmer, covered, for 5 minutes.

Dissolve the cornstarch in the water in a small bowl. Stir into the meatball mixture. Add the bell pepper. Simmer, uncovered, for 5 minutes or until the vegetables are tender. Serve over rice.

Yield: 6 servings

GOLDEN CATFISH FILLETS

1	egg white
1	cup milk
1	cup cornmeal
3/4	teaspoon salt
1/4	teaspoon garlic powder
1/4	to 1/2 teaspoon cayenne pepper
4	(8-ounce) catfish fillets
	Vegetable oil for frying

Beat the egg white in a shallow bowl until foamy. Add the milk and mix well.

Combine the cornmeal, salt, garlic powder and cayenne pepper in another shallow bowl. Dip the fish fillets in the milk mixture, then in the cornmeal mixture to coat.

Pour the oil into a large skillet to a 1/4-inch depth. Heat over medium-high heat until hot. Fry the fish fillets in the hot oil for 3 to 4 minutes per side or until it flakes easily. Garnish with lemon wedges.

Yield: 4 servings

CODY'S SEAFOOD GUMBO "LOUISIANA STYLE"

2 tablespoons each vegetable oil and water
4 cups okra, cut into 1/2-inch pieces
2/3 cup vegetable oil
1/2 cup flour
2 medium onions, chopped
2 ribs celery, chopped
1 green bell pepper, chopped
1/4 cup chopped fresh parsley
2 garlic cloves, minced
1 (16-ounce) can stewed tomatoes
   Shrimp Stock (at right)
4 to 5 medium crabs, cut into quarters
2 bay leaves
7 1/2 teaspoons Worcestershire sauce
1 1/2 teaspoons each Creole seasoning and hot red pepper sauce
1 teaspoon salt
3/4 teaspoon black pepper
1/2 teaspoon cayenne pepper
2 pounds peeled deveined shrimp
   Hot cooked rice

MAKING SHRIMP STOCK

To make your own Shrimp Stock, rinse the shells from 2 pounds of shrimp and place in a large saucepan. Add 10 cups of water. Bring to a boil. Simmer for 1 hour. Strain and discard the shells.

Heat 2 tablespoons oil and 2 tablespoons water in a heavy skillet. Add the okra. Sauté for 30 minutes or until tender; set aside.

Heat 2/3 cup oil in a Dutch oven. Add the flour and cook to form a brown roux, stirring constantly. Add the onions, celery, bell pepper, parsley and garlic. Sauté until the vegetables are tender. Stir in the tomatoes. Cook for 15 minutes.

Add the okra, Shrimp Stock, crabs (including claws) and next 7 ingredients. Bring to a boil over medium-low heat. Reduce the heat to low. Simmer for about 2 hours, stirring occasionally. Stir in the shrimp. Cook until the shrimp turn pink. Remove and discard the bay leaves. Serve over rice. Prepare 1 day in advance for enhanced flavor.

Yield: 8 servings

BLACK-EYED PEA HOPPIN' JOHN

2¹/2 cups water
1   cup dried black-eyed peas
1¹/2 teaspoons salt
1   teaspoon crushed red pepper
1   bay leaf
2   tablespoons cider vinegar
1   tablespoon vegetable oil
1   tablespoon finely diced red bell pepper
1   tablespoon finely diced green bell pepper
1   tablespoon finely diced red onion
1   tablespoon finely diced celery
1   teaspoon minced garlic
1   teaspoon thyme (fresh or dried)
   Salt and black pepper to taste

Place the water, black-eyed peas, salt, crushed red pepper and bay leaf in a heavy saucepan. Bring to a boil over high heat. Reduce the heat to low. Simmer for 45 minutes to 1 hour or until the peas are tender but not split. Remove from the heat; drain. Stir in the vinegar. Remove and discard the bay leaf. Cover and keep warm.

Heat the oil in a medium skillet over high heat. Add the bell peppers, onion, celery, garlic and thyme. Sauté for 2 to 3 minutes or until the vegetables are tender but not browned. Season with salt and black pepper. Stir into the warm black-eyed peas.

Yield: 4 servings

TANGY MARINATED CARROTS

2 pounds sliced carrots, cooked, drained
1 medium onion, sliced
1 medium green bell pepper, sliced into rings
1 (10-ounce) can tomato soup
1 cup sugar
3/4 cup white vinegar
1/3 to 1/2 cup vegetable oil
1 teaspoon salt
1 teaspoon pepper
1 teaspoon dry mustard
1 teaspoon Worcestershire sauce

Layer the cooled carrots, onion and bell pepper in a large bowl.

Combine the soup, sugar, vinegar, oil, salt, pepper, dry mustard and Worcestershire sauce in a medium bowl. Pour over the vegetables. Marinate in the refrigerator for 24 hours.

Yield: 16 servings

CORN PUDDING

1   (15-ounce) can cream-style corn
1   (11-ounce) can whole kernel corn
1   cup milk
3   eggs
3   tablespoons flour
3   tablespoons sugar
2   tablespoons butter, softened
1/2 teaspoon salt
     Dash of pepper

Combine the cream-style corn, whole kernel corn, milk, eggs, flour, sugar, butter, salt and pepper in a bowl and mix well. Pour into a greased 1 1/2-quart baking dish. Bake at 325 degrees for 1 hour or until a knife inserted near the center comes out clean.

Yield: 6 servings

ROSEMARY POTATOES

1/2 cup olive oil
6   sprigs of fresh rosemary, chopped, or 2 tablespoons
     crushed dried rosemary
3   garlic cloves, crushed or minced
1 1/2 teaspoons salt
     Freshly ground pepper to taste
10   small or 6 medium red potatoes, sliced 1/8 inch thick

Combine the olive oil, rosemary, garlic, salt and pepper in a bowl and mix well. Add the potatoes. Toss until evenly coated.

Spread the potato mixture in a 9×13-inch baking dish. Bake at 350 degrees for 35 minutes or until tender.

Yield: 6 servings

MURIEL GRAY'S SQUASH CASSEROLE

2   *pounds fresh or frozen squash, chopped*
1   *small onion, finely chopped*
3   *tablespoons (heaping) flour*
1   *teaspoon salt*
1/2 *teaspoon sugar*
2   *eggs, lightly beaten*
1   *cup milk*
3   *tablespoons margarine, melted*
8   *ounces shredded cheese*

If using frozen squash, thaw and drain it. Combine the squash, onion, flour, salt and sugar in a bowl and mix well. Add the eggs, milk and margarine. Stir in the cheese. Spoon into a greased 9×13-inch baking dish.

Bake at 375 degrees for 40 minutes or until a knife inserted near the center comes out clean. Serve immediately.

Note: Casserole may be topped with buttered bread crumbs after baking for 40 minutes. Bake for 10 minutes longer to brown the topping.

Yield: 12 servings

$\mathcal{J}$O-DIE-FOR CHOCOLATE PECAN PIE

1/2   *cup (1 stick) butter or margarine, melted*
3   *cups sugar*
1   *(12-ounce) can evaporated milk*
4   *eggs*
7   *tablespoons baking cocoa*
1   *tablespoon vanilla extract*
    Pinch of salt
2   *cups flaked coconut*
1   *cup chopped pecans*
3   *unbaked (8-inch) pie shells*

Beat the butter, sugar, evaporated milk, eggs, baking cocoa, vanilla and salt in a mixing bowl at low speed. Stir in the coconut and pecans.

Divide the filling evenly among the pie shells. Bake at 350 degrees for 45 minutes or until a knife inserted near the centers comes out clean.

Yield: 18 servings

TROPHY COOKIES

2 1/4 cups flour
1 teaspoon baking soda
1 teaspoon salt
1 cup (2 sticks) butter, softened
3/4 cup sugar
3/4 cup packed brown sugar
1 teaspoon vanilla extract
1/4 teaspoon butter flavoring
2 eggs
2 cups chocolate chips
1 cup white chocolate chips
1 cup toffee bits
1 cup rolled oats
1 cup chopped nuts (optional)

Combine the flour, baking soda and salt in a bowl and mix well.

Cream the butter, sugar, brown sugar, vanilla and butter flavoring in a mixing bowl until light and fluffy. Add the eggs 1 at a time, mixing well after each addition. Add the flour mixture gradually and mix well. Stir in the chocolate chips, white chocolate chips, toffee bits, oats and nuts.

Drop by rounded teaspoonfuls 2 inches apart onto a nonstick cookie sheet. Bake at 375 degrees for 9 to 12 minutes or until golden brown. Cool on the cookie sheet for 3 minutes. Remove to a wire rack to cool completely.

Yield: 6 dozen

HOLE-IN-ONE PEANUT BUTTER COOKIES

1   cup (2 sticks) butter, softened
1   cup peanut butter
1 1/2 cups sugar
2   eggs
1   teaspoon vanilla extract
1 1/4 cups self-rising flour

Cream the butter, peanut butter and sugar in a mixing bowl until light and fluffy. Beat in the eggs and vanilla. Add the flour and mix well.

Drop by teaspoonfuls 2 inches apart onto an ungreased cookie sheet. Bake at 350 degrees for 15 minutes or until golden brown. Cool on a wire rack.

Yield: 4 dozen

SUMMER

A SULTRY SUMMER DAY

New Bern's coastal heritage is more powerful than ever during its long summer season. During centuries past, large sailing vessels and wooden crafts plied her rivers. Gangs of boys roamed the wharves fronting the Neuse and Trent Rivers and learned to swim by diving off the menhaden boats that came into the shipyard. Nursemaids and mothers visited with one another as they pushed their baby carriages through Union Point Park and along the water's edge.

Hatteras

On the Back Porch
PAGE 65

Sand in Our Shoes—
A day at the Beach
PAGE 76

From the Family Garden
PAGE 92

Kenneth Morris Insurance

On the Back Porch

On the Back Porch

Beverages
Barbara's Summer Refresher
Claire's Lemonade Stand Lemonade

Appetizers
Carolina Crab Meat Appetizer
Grilled Shrimp Appetizer

Salad
Creamy Orange Pineapple Salad

Main Dishes
Grilled Lamb Chops
Cape Lookout Baked Flounder
Grilled Salmon with Lemon Caper Sauce
New Orleans Shrimp Creole

Side Dishes
Back Porch Black Bean and Monterey Jack Cheese Casserole
Green Onion Potato Casserole

Desserts
Max's Blueberry Crisp
Piña Colada Cake
Strawberry Cake
Easy Orange Sherbet

 BARBARA'S SUMMER REFRESHER

3¹/2 cups water
2   cups vodka
1   (12-ounce) can frozen lemonade concentrate, thawed
1   (12-ounce) can frozen limeade concentrate, thawed
1   (6-ounce) can frozen orange juice concentrate, thawed
¹/2 cup sugar
2   (32-ounce) bottles lemon-lime soda

Combine the water, vodka, lemonade concentrate, limeade concentrate, orange juice concentrate and sugar in a bowl and mix well. Pour into a freezer container. Freeze, covered, for 8 hours.

Spoon the frozen slush into glasses, filling them halfway. Pour in enough soda to fill the glasses.

Yield: 16 servings

CLAIRE'S LEMONADE STAND LEMONADE

Juice of 12 lemons (about 2 to 2¹/2 cups)
2   cups sugar
12   cups cold water, or to taste

Combine the lemon juice and sugar in a large pitcher. Add the water, stirring until the sugar is completely dissolved. Serve over ice. Garnish with fresh lemon slices.

Yield: 14 (8-ounce) servings

At the turn of the twentieth century, New Bern's agricultural and industrial preeminence was celebrated with a series of spectaculars at the fairgrounds on George Street.

CAROLINA CRAB MEAT APPETIZER

8   ounces cream cheese, softened
1/2 to 1 small Vidalia onion, chopped
2   to 3 teaspoons Worcestershire sauce
1   (12-ounce) bottle cocktail sauce
2   cups fresh crab meat

Combine the cream cheese, onion and Worcestershire sauce in a bowl and mix well. Spread over the bottom of a shallow 1-quart serving dish. Top with the cocktail sauce and crab meat. Chill for 6 to 8 hours. Serve with assorted crackers.

Yield: 32 (2-tablespoon) servings

GRILLED SHRIMP APPETIZER

2   pounds medium or large deveined peeled shrimp
1/4 cup olive oil
1   tablespoon minced garlic
1/2 cup dried seasoned fine bread crumbs
1/4 cup chopped fresh parsley
     Salt and pepper to taste

Soak 10- or 12-inch skewers in water for 30 minutes; drain.

Combine the shrimp, olive oil and garlic in a bowl and toss to coat the shrimp. Add the bread crumbs and parsley and toss to coat the shrimp. Season with salt and pepper.

Thread the shrimp onto the skewers. Chill, covered, for up to 3 hours. Grill over medium-hot coals for 4 minutes or until shrimp turn pink. Serve with cocktail sauce or lemon wasabi sauce.

Yield: 4 to 6 servings

CREAMY ORANGE PINEAPPLE SALAD

1   (8-ounce) can crushed pineapple
1   (3-ounce) package orange gelatin
3   ounces cream cheese
1   cup whipping cream
1   carrot, shredded (1/3 cup)

Drain the pineapple, reserving the juice. Add enough water to the juice to measure 1 cup.

Place the gelatin and cream cheese in a heatproof mixing bowl. Bring the juice mixture to a boil in a saucepan. Pour over the gelatin and cream cheese. Beat until smooth. Cool, stirring occasionally.

Whip the cream in a mixing bowl. Fold the whipped cream, carrot and pineapple into the cooled gelatin mixture. Pour into 8 to 12 individual molds. Chill until firm.

Yield: 8 to 12 servings

GRILLED LAMB CHOPS

2   tablespoons Dijonnaise
1   tablespoon reduced-sodium soy sauce
1¹/2 teaspoons fresh cracked pepper
2   garlic cloves, crushed
6   to 8 (1- to 1¹/2-inch) lamb chops

Combine the Dijonnaise, soy sauce, pepper and garlic in a bowl and mix well; set aside.

Grill the lamb chops over medium coals until partially cooked. Coat with the soy sauce mixture. Grill to taste.

Yield: 6 to 8 servings

CAPE LOOKOUT BAKED FLOUNDER

1   (3-pound) flounder
    Salt to taste
    Cornmeal
3   slices bacon, chopped
6   medium potatoes, sliced
1   small onion, sliced
3   tomatoes, sliced

Cut slits along the length of the flounder at 1-inch intervals. Season with salt and sprinkle with cornmeal. Insert the bacon into the slits. Place the fish in a greased baking pan. Bake at 350 degrees for 10 minutes.

Arrange the potatoes and onion around the fish. Season the vegetables with salt. Bake, covered, for 20 to 30 minutes.

Reduce the oven temperature to 325 degrees. Add the tomatoes. Bake for 30 minutes or until the fish flakes easily.

Yield: 6 servings

After a morning of parades and an afternoon of historic homes touring, on June 11, 1929, buffet suppers were scheduled for 6 p.m. Barbecued spareribs and Carolina crab cakes, followed by a variety of pies, fortified a crowd of 8,000 who watched "New Bern in Historical Review." Thus began the tradition of portraying historical characters still carried on today at Tryon Palace Historic Sites and Gardens. New Bern still celebrates its seasons and its coastal heritage whenever an occasion arises.

GRILLED SALMON WITH LEMON CAPER SAUCE

FISH MARINADE

1/4 cup fresh parsley
    leaves, minced
1/4 cup fresh basil
    leaves, minced
2   large shallots,
    minced
1/3 cup extra-virgin
    olive oil
1/3 cup vegetable oil

Combine the parsley,
basil, shallots, olive oil
and vegetable oil in a
bowl and mix well.

4   salmon fillets
    Fish Marinade (at left)
1/4 cup fish stock
1/4 cup dry white wine
2 1/2 tablespoons fresh lemon juice
1/4 cup heavy cream
1   anchovy fillet
1   teaspoon Dijon mustard
6   tablespoons unsalted butter, softened
1 1/2 tablespoons capers, drained
    Salt to taste
    Cayenne pepper to taste

Combine the salmon and Fish Marinade in a large sealable plastic bag. Seal the bag, pressing out any air. Turn the bag over several times to coat the fish with the marinade. Marinate in the refrigerator for 2 hours or longer, turning the bag over occasionally.

Cook the stock, wine and lemon juice in a 1-quart nonreactive saucepan for 12 minutes or until the liquid is reduced to 2 tablespoons. Add the cream. Boil for 2 to 3 minutes or until the liquid is reduced to 1/4 cup.

Purée the cream sauce with the anchovy and mustard in a blender. Return the sauce to the pan. Whisk in the butter, 1 tablespoon at a time. Remove from the heat. Stir in 1 tablespoon of the capers, salt and cayenne pepper to taste. Keep the sauce warm.

Remove the fish from the marinade and gently pat dry with a paper towel. Discard the marinade. Arrange the fish on a broiler pan, skin side down. Broil 8 inches from the heat source for 8 minutes or until the fish flakes easily. Do not overcook.

Spoon about 2 tablespoons warm sauce over each fillet. Garnish with the remaining 1/2 tablespoon capers.

Yield: 4 servings

NEW ORLEANS SHRIMP CREOLE

2   tablespoons olive oil
3   green bell peppers, finely chopped
2   onions, finely chopped
1   garlic clove, minced
2   cups stewed or canned tomatoes
1   teaspoon paprika
    Dash of Tabasco sauce
    Salt and pepper to taste
1 1/2 pounds fresh deveined peeled shrimp
    Hot cooked rice

Heat the olive oil in a large skillet over medium-low heat. Add the bell peppers, onions and garlic. Cook over low heat until tender, stirring frequently. Add the tomatoes. Simmer for 30 minutes.

Stir in the paprika and Tabasco sauce. Season with salt and pepper. Stir in the shrimp. Cook for 5 minutes or until the shrimp turn pink. Serve with rice.

Yield: 6 servings

BACK PORCH BLACK BEAN AND MONTEREY JACK CHEESE CASSEROLE

1 1/4 cups water
1/2 cup uncooked rice
    Dash of salt
1 1/2 cups diced onions
1 cup each diced green and red bell pepper
2 teaspoons minced garlic
2 tablespoons vegetable oil
1 cup each dry white wine and chicken or vegetable broth
1 cup each golden raisins and slivered blanched almonds
4 teaspoons cumin
1/4 teaspoon crushed red pepper
1/4 teaspoon salt, or to taste
2 dashes of coarsely ground black pepper
    Seasoned Black Beans (at left)
    Salt to taste
4 cups shredded Monterey Jack cheese
1/4 cup dry bread crumbs

Bring the water to a boil in a small saucepan. Stir in the rice and dash of salt. Reduce the heat to low. Cook, covered, for 15 minutes or until the rice is tender and all the water is absorbed. Remove from the heat.

Sauté the onions, bell peppers and garlic in hot oil in a skillet until tender. Add the rice, sautéed vegetables, wine, broth, raisins, almonds, cumin, crushed red pepper, 1/4 teaspoon salt, black pepper and Seasoned Black Beans in a large saucepan and mix well. Cook over low heat for 8 to 10 minutes or until the mixture begins to thicken. Season with salt.

Cover the bottom and sides of a buttered 10×13-inch baking dish with 3 1/4 cups of the cheese. Spoon the bean mixture over the cheese. Top with the remaining 3/4 cup cheese and bread crumbs. Bake at 375 degrees for 30 to 35 minutes or until the top is crusty and the beans are bubbly.

Yield: 6 to 8 servings

GREEN ONION POTATO CASSEROLE

6   *medium or 4 large potatoes, peeled, cut into quarters*
1   *cup sour cream*
1   *cup shredded sharp Cheddar cheese*
6   *to 8 green onions, chopped*
1   *teaspoon salt*
1/3 *cup butter, melted*

Place the potatoes with enough water to cover in a saucepan. Boil just until tender. Drain and cool. Coarsely shred the potatoes. Place in a large bowl.

Add the sour cream, cheese, green onions and salt and mix gently. Spoon into a greased 2-quart baking dish. Drizzle the butter over the top.

Bake at 400 degrees for 30 minutes or until golden brown.

Yield: 6 to 8 servings

MAX'S BLUEBERRY CRISP

4 cups fresh
blueberries
1/3 cup sugar
2 teaspoons
lemon juice
1/4 cup (1/2 stick)
butter, softened
1/3 cup packed
brown sugar
1/3 cup flour
1/4 cup quick-
cooking oats

Place the blueberries in
a greased 1 1/2-quart-
deep baking dish.
Sprinkle the sugar and
lemon juice over the
berries. Beat the butter
and brown sugar in a
bowl until light and
fluffy. Stir in the flour
and oats. Spread over
the blueberries. Bake
at 350 degrees for 40
minutes. Serve with
whipped cream or
ice cream.

PIÑA COLADA CAKE

1   (2-layer) package yellow cake mix
1 1/2 cups water
1/2   cup vegetable oil
2   eggs
1 1/2 cups flaked coconut
1   (6-ounce) package vanilla instant pudding mix
12   ounces whipped topping
1   (15-ounce) can cream of coconut

Beat the cake mix, water, oil and eggs in a mixing bowl until well blended. Stir in the coconut. Pour into 2 greased and floured 9-inch round cake pans.

Bake at 350 degrees for 25 to 30 minutes or until the layers test done. Cool in the pans for 10 minutes. Remove to wire racks to cool completely.

Prepare the pudding mix according to the package directions. Chill until set. Add half the whipped topping to the prepared pudding and mix well.

Place 1 cake layer in the bottom of a trifle dish. Punch holes in the top of the cake. Top with half the cream of coconut, the pudding mixture and second cake layer. Punch holes in the top of the second cake. Top with the remaining cream of coconut and whipped topping. Refrigerate for 8 hours or longer before serving.

Yield: 15 servings

STRAWBERRY CAKE

Cake

1   (2-layer) package white cake mix
1   (3-ounce) package strawberry gelatin
1   cup vegetable oil
1/2 cup milk
4   eggs
1   cup chopped strawberries
1   cup chopped pecans
1   cup flaked coconut

Strawberry Frosting

1/2 cup (1 stick) margarine, softened
3   ounces cream cheese, softened
1   (1-pound) package confectioners' sugar
1/2 cup chopped strawberries
1/2 cup chopped pecans
1/2 cup flaked coconut

For the cake, beat the cake mix, gelatin, oil, milk and eggs in a mixing bowl for 2 minutes. Stir in the strawberries, pecans and coconut. Pour into 3 greased and floured 8-inch round cake pans. Bake at 350 degrees for 25 minutes or until the layers test done. Cool in the pans for 10 minutes. Remove to wire racks to cool completely.

For the frosting, cream the margarine, cream cheese and confectioners' sugar in a mixing bowl until light and fluffy. Stir in the strawberries, pecans and coconut. Spread the frosting between the layers and over the top and side of the cooled cake. Refrigerate the frosted cake until ready to serve.

Yield: 12 servings

EASY ORANGE SHERBET

1   (14-ounce) can sweetened condensed milk
1   (8-ounce) can crushed pineapple
1   (64-ounce) bottle orange soda

Pour the condensed milk, pineapple and orange soda into an ice cream freezer container. Freeze using manufacturer's directions.

Sand in Our Shoes—
A Day at the Beach

Beverage
Fish House Punch

Appetizers
Angels on Horseback • Layered Seafood Tray
Summery Minted Mango Salsa • Seven-Layer Dip

Salads
Spicy Sesame and Ginger Noodle Salad
Strawberry Pretzel Salad
Frisée, Radicchio and Mixed Greens with Shrimp

Main Dishes
London Broil • Island Grilled Swordfish
Crab Cakes with Chardonnay Cream Sauce
Louisiana Crayfish Boil
Shrimp Tortellini • Seafood Thermidor

Side Dishes
Sesame Asparagus
Cauliflower Italiano
Confetti Corn • Rice Oriental

Desserts
Caribbean Coconut Cream Pie
Poppy Seed Cake
Seafoam Cookies

Fish House Punch

1 1/2 cups sugar
8   cups water
8   cups Jamaican rum
4   cups Cognac
4   cups lemon juice
1/2 cup peach brandy

Dissolve the sugar in the water in a large bowl. Stir in the rum, Cognac, lemon juice and brandy. Let stand for 2 hours at room temperature to allow the flavors to mellow; stir occasionally. Pour over ice in a punch bowl to serve.

Yield: 30 servings

Angels on Horseback

12   slices bacon, cut into halves
1   pint oysters, well drained
     Salt and pepper to taste
     Paprika to taste
1   bunch fresh parsley (optional)

Wrap a piece of bacon around each oyster, securing with a wooden pick. Season with salt, pepper and paprika. Place on a rack in a shallow baking pan.

Bake at 350 degrees for 15 to 20 minutes or until browned. Serve on a bed of parsley.

Yield: 6 servings

LAYERED SEAFOOD TRAY

8   ounces cream cheese, softened
1/2 cup sour cream
1/4 teaspoon salt
     Dash of cayenne pepper
     Dash of lemon pepper
1   (12-ounce) bottle cocktail sauce, chilled
8   ounces crab meat
8   ounces shrimp, cooked, diced

Combine the cream cheese, sour cream, salt, cayenne pepper and lemon pepper in a bowl and mix well. Spread in the center of a serving plate, forming a circle. Refrigerate, covered, for at least 30 minutes.

When ready to serve, spread the cocktail sauce over the cream cheese circle. Top with the crab meat and shrimp. Serve with crackers.

Yield: 30 (2-tablespoon) servings

SUMMERY MINTED MANGO SALSA

2   mangoes, finely chopped
2/3 cup finely chopped red bell pepper
2/3 cup finely chopped red onion
2/3 cup finely chopped tomato
2   tablespoons chopped fresh mint
2   tablespoons lime juice
1   tablespoon rice wine vinegar

Combine the mangoes, bell pepper, onion, tomato, mint, lime juice and vinegar in a bowl and mix well. Serve with grilled fish or chicken.

Note: Salsa may be blended in a food processor.

Yield: 24 (2-tablespoon) servings

SEVEN-LAYER DIP

2   cups sour cream
1/4 cup chopped onion
1   (16-ounce) jar salsa
8   ounces shredded Cheddar cheese
8   ounces shredded mozzarella or pepper Jack cheese
1/4 cup chopped tomato
1/4 cup chopped green bell pepper
1/4 cup sliced black olives

Layer the sour cream, onion, salsa, Cheddar cheese and mozzarella cheese in a 10-inch square pan. Layer the tomato, bell pepper and olives over the layers. Serve with nacho chips.

Yield: 72 (2-tablespoon) servings

RAFTING UP

Boats gather on the rivers and raft together to form a floating picnic on the water. Summery Minted Mango Salsa and the Layered Seafood Tray are perfect accompaniments to a day spent floating on the river.

SPICY SESAME AND GINGER NOODLE SALAD

3/4 cup low-sodium soy sauce
9 tablespoons fresh lemon juice
6 tablespoons minced gingerroot
6 tablespoons tahini
1/4 cup honey
2 teaspoons crushed red pepper
6 tablespoons sesame oil
3 (8-ounce) packages thin yellow Japanese noodles
 Salt to taste
12 ounces snow peas, trimmed
1 1/2 bunches green onions
6 medium carrots, julienned
3 red bell peppers, julienned
1 1/2 cucumbers, peeled, seeded, julienned
 Black pepper to taste
1/4 cup sesame seeds, toasted

Whisk the soy sauce, lemon juice, gingerroot, tahini, honey and crushed red pepper in a bowl. Whisk in 3 tablespoons of the sesame oil; set aside.

Cook the noodles in a saucepan of boiling salted water for 5 minutes or just until tender yet firm to the bite; drain. Place in a large bowl. Toss with the remaining 3 tablespoons sesame oil.

Cut the snow peas and green onions diagonally into thin slices. Add the snow peas, green onions, carrots, bell peppers and cucumbers to the noodles, tossing to mix. Pour the soy sauce dressing over the top and toss again. Season with salt and black pepper. Sprinkle with the sesame seeds.

Yield: 14 servings

STRAWBERRY PRETZEL SALAD

2   cups coarsely chopped pretzels
3/4   cup (1¹/2 sticks) butter, melted
3   tablespoons sugar
8   ounces cream cheese, softened
1   cup sugar
8   ounces whipped topping
1   (6-ounce) package strawberry gelatin
2   cups boiling water
2   (10-ounce) packages frozen strawberries

Combine the pretzels, butter and 3 tablespoons sugar in a bowl and mix well. Press over the bottom of a 9×13-inch baking pan. Bake at 400 degrees for 8 to 10 minutes. Cool completely.

Beat the cream cheese and 1 cup sugar in a mixing bowl until well blended. Fold in the whipped topping. Spread over the cooled crust.

Dissolve the gelatin in the boiling water in a bowl. Stir in the frozen strawberries. Let stand until the gelatin is partially set. Spoon evenly over the cream cheese layer. Refrigerate, covered, until set.

Yield: 12 servings

Every summer on the Fourth of July weekend, the Eastern Carolina Yacht Club sponsors a trip to Ocracoke, a small barrier island approximately 5 nautical miles across the Pamlico Sound from New Bern. The notorious pirate Blackbeard terrorized these waters during the 18th century. He may have feasted on Frogmore Stew as do the Yacht Club members. (One nautical mile equals 6076.12 feet an hour, to average a speed of 10 knots. The barrier islands are approximately 50 knots from New Bern.)

FRISÉE, RADICCHIO AND MIXED GREENS WITH SHRIMP

3   tablespoons raspberry vinegar
3   tablespoons minced fresh tarragon
2   tablespoons minced shallots
2/3 cup extra-virgin olive oil
    Salt and pepper to taste
2   tablespoons extra-virgin olive oil
12 ounces assorted wild mushrooms (such as cremini and stemmed
    shiitake), sliced
1   pound cooked large shrimp, peeled
6   cups mixed baby greens
4   cups bite-size frisée or curly endive pieces
1   head radicchio, torn into bite-size pieces

Whisk the vinegar, tarragon and shallots in a small bowl until well mixed. Whisk in 2/3 cup olive oil gradually. Season with salt and pepper.

Heat 2 tablespoons olive oil in a large nonstick skillet over medium-high heat. Add the mushrooms. Sauté for 10 minutes or until tender. Season with salt and pepper. Cool.

Combine the shrimp, baby greens, frisée, radicchio and mushrooms in a large bowl. Add the vinaigrette and toss to coat. Season with salt and pepper.

Note: Vinaigrette may be prepared up to 1 day ahead of time. Cover and chill. Bring to room temperature and whisk before using.

Yield: 10 servings

LONDON BROIL

1 1/2 pounds London broil
Beach Marinade (at right)

Pierce the surface of the London broil gently with a fork to tenderize. Place the beef and Beach Marinade in a large sealable plastic bag. Marinate in the refrigerator for 2 to 12 hours; drain. Grill over hot coals for 6 minutes on each side or until done to taste. Slice on the diagonal.

Yield: 6 servings

ISLAND GRILLED SWORDFISH

1/2 cup soy sauce
1/4 cup sherry
2   teaspoons minced garlic
1   teaspoon grated gingerroot
4   (4- to 6-ounce) swordfish steaks
1/4 cup (1/2 stick) butter, softened
1   tablespoon minced shallots
1   teaspoon chopped fresh parsley

Mix the soy sauce, sherry, garlic and gingerroot in a bowl. Pour into a large sealable plastic bag. Add the swordfish to the marinade in the bag and seal. Turn the bag over several times to coat the fish. Marinate in the refrigerator for 1 hour, turning the fish over after 30 minutes. Cream the butter with the shallots and parsley in a bowl. Cover and set aside.

Remove the swordfish from the marinade, reserving the marinade. Place the reserved marinade in a small saucepan. Bring to a boil. Boil for 2 to 3 minutes, stirring constantly. Grill the fish over hot coals until it flakes easily, basting with the marinade; do not overcook. Top each steak with one-fourth of the seasoned butter.

Yield: 4 servings

BEACH MARINADE

1/2 cup soy sauce
1/4 cup ketchup
     Juice of 1 lemon
3   tablespoons Worcestershire sauce
4   scallions, chopped
1   large garlic clove, sliced
     Pepper to taste

Combine the soy sauce, ketchup, lemon juice, Worcestershire sauce, scallions, garlic and pepper in a bowl and mix well

Note: May substitute balsamic vinegar for the ketchup.

CRAB CAKES WITH CHARDONNAY CREAM SAUCE

CHARDONNAY CREAM SAUCE

1³/4 cups chardonnay
   or other dry
   white wine
1/3 cup chopped
   shallots
1 cup heavy cream
   Salt and pepper
   to taste

Boil the wine with the shallots in a heavy medium saucepan for 10 minutes or until the liquid is reduced to 1/2 cup. Stir in the cream. Boil for 10 minutes or until the liquid is reduced to a sauce consistency. Season with salt and pepper.

1¹/2 pounds crab meat, drained (about 4 cups)
2¹/2 cups finely crushed potato chips
1¹/4 cups fresh bread crumbs (prepared from French bread)
1 (7-ounce) jar roasted red peppers, drained, coarsely chopped
1/2 cup thinly sliced green onions
2 eggs
2 tablespoons chopped fresh dill
1 tablespoon Dijon mustard
1 tablespoon whole-grain mustard
1 tablespoon mayonnaise
1/4 cup (about) vegetable oil
   Chardonnay Cream Sauce (at left)

Combine the crab meat, 1/2 cup of the potato chips, bread crumbs, roasted peppers, green onions, eggs, dill, Dijon mustard, whole-grain mustard and mayonnaise in a large bowl and mix well. Shape into sixteen 2¹/2-inch-diameter cakes, using 1/4 cup of the crab mixture for each cake. Place the remaining 2 cups potato chips in a shallow dish. Press each crab cake into the chips, turning to coat evenly.

Heat 2 tablespoons of the oil in a large heavy skillet over medium-high heat. Add the crab cakes, a few at a time. Cook for 5 minutes per side or until golden brown and heated through, adding more oil as necessary. Drain on paper towels.

Place 4 crab cakes in the center of each plate. Spoon the Chardonnay Cream Sauce around the cakes and serve immediately.

Note: The sauce and uncooked crab cakes may be prepared up to 6 hours ahead of time. Refrigerate, covered, in separate containers. Rewarm the sauce over medium-low heat, stirring occasionally. Cook the crab cakes as directed.

Yield: 4 servings

LOUISIANA CRAYFISH BOIL

30   pounds crayfish
3   (26-ounce) boxes salt
2   cups cayenne pepper
1/2   cup liquid crab boil
1/4   cup crushed red pepper
8   lemons, cut into quarters
3   heads garlic, cut into halves
2   yellow onions, cut into halves
1   bunch celery, coarsely chopped
      Lagniappe: new potatoes, corn on the cob, smoked sausage, artichokes, mushrooms

Rinse the crayfish with a hose if they are muddy; do not soak. The crayfish do not need to be purged.

Add enough water to a 50- to 60-quart pot to cover the crayfish when they are added. The pot should have a basket insert so the crayfish can be easily removed. Bring the water to a rapid boil. Add the salt, cayenne, crab boil, crushed red pepper, lemons, garlic, onions, celery and lagniappe. Boil for at least 10 minutes to allow the flavors to blend. When the vegetables are almost cooked, add the crayfish. Return to a boil. Boil for 2 minutes. Turn off the heat. Cover and let stand for 25 to 30 minutes to allow the crayfish to soak up the seasonings. Empty the basket on a large table and dig in.

For successive boils, use the same cooking water. For the second boil, add half the amounts of salt, cayenne, crab boil and crushed red pepper; for any additional boils, reduce these seasonings by two-thirds. Replenish full amounts of lemons, garlic, onions, celery and lagniappe ingredients each time.

Note: The lagniappe ingredients listed are only suggestions. Substitute any ingredients you like. Be sure to use a high-powered flame for the heat source and allow plenty of time for preparation.

Yield: 60 servings

To eat a crayfish, first break off the head. Suck the juice from inside the head if you'd like. Then remove the top shell fragment, pinch the tail, and squeeze out the meat.

SHRIMP TORTELLINI

1   (9-ounce) package fresh cheese tortellini
1/3 cup butter or margarine
1   pound fresh deveined peeled medium shrimp
1   shallot, minced
2   tablespoons chopped fresh basil, or 2 teaspoons dried basil
1/2 cup grated Parmesan cheese

Cook the tortellini according to the package directions. Drain and set aside.

Melt the butter in a large skillet over medium-high heat. Add the shrimp, shallot and basil. Cook for 5 minutes or until the shrimp turn pink, stirring constantly. Add the tortellini and Parmesan cheese. Toss gently. Garnish with additional fresh basil leaves.

Yield: 4 servings

SEAFOOD THERMIDOR

3   *pounds fresh deveined peeled shrimp*
1   *tablespoon Old Bay seasoning or crab boil*
      Butter
1 1/2 *pounds mushrooms, sliced*
3   *garlic cloves, crushed*
3/4 *cup flour*
3   *cups (or more) chicken broth*
2   *cups (or more) light cream*
1   *cup (or more) heavy cream*
2   *tablespoons prepared mustard*
1   *tablespoon salt*
1   *tablespoon lemon juice*
      Few drops of Tabasco sauce
5   *lobster tails, cooked, cut into bite-size pieces*
1   *pound crab meat*
1/4 *cup dry sherry*
1   *cup grated Parmesan cheese*

Cook the shrimp with the seasoning in simmering water in a saucepan until they turn pink. Drain and cool.

Melt a small amount of butter in a large saucepan. Add the mushrooms. Cook gently until tender. Stir in the garlic and flour, mixing well. Add the chicken broth, light cream and heavy cream gradually. Cook until smooth and thickened, stirring constantly. Add the mustard, salt, lemon juice and Tabasco sauce. Stir in the shrimp, lobster and crab meat. (The seafood mixture may be packed in pint containers at this point and frozen. Thaw in the refrigerator before reheating.)

Spoon into a 3 1/2-quart baking dish. Bake at 350 degrees for 40 minutes. Remove from the oven. Stir in the sherry, adding additional cream or chicken broth to make of the desired consistency. Sprinkle with the Parmesan cheese. Bake until thick and bubbly.

Yield: 12 to 14 servings

For six months of the year, beginning in April, the rivers became the playground for children and teens, giving them a freedom seldom found for the youth of present day. Crab lines working for the evening's meal were thrown from docks, and little runabouts filled with teens racing for their freedom sprinted across the rivers on a summer's day...

SESAME ASPARAGUS

1 pound fresh asparagus, trimmed, cut diagonally into thirds
1/2 teaspoon vegetable oil
1/2 cup finely diced red bell pepper
1 tablespoon low-sodium soy sauce
1/2 teaspoon sesame oil
2 teaspoons sesame seeds, toasted

Cook the asparagus in enough boiling water to cover in a saucepan for 3 minutes or until tender-crisp. Drain and rinse under cold water; drain well.

Heat the vegetable oil in a nonstick skillet. Add the bell pepper. Cook for 1 minute. Stir in the asparagus. Cook for 2 minutes or until heated through. Add the soy sauce and sesame oil. Toss with the vegetables. Remove to a serving platter. Sprinkle with the sesame seeds.

Yield: 4 servings

CAULIFLOWER ITALIANO

1 head cauliflower, separated into florets, or 1 (16-ounce) bag frozen cauliflower
4 to 8 ounces cherry tomatoes, cut into quarters
Italian Salad Dressing to taste (at left)

Cook the cauliflower in enough boiling water to cover in a saucepan until tender; drain. Combine the cauliflower, cherry tomatoes and Italian Salad Dressing in a bowl and mix well.

Yield: 6 servings

CONFETTI CORN

2 cups fresh corn kernels
3/4 cup water
1 (14-ounce) can black beans, rinsed, drained
2 small cucumbers, seeded, chopped
1 red bell pepper, chopped
1/2 cup sliced green onions
1/4 cup chopped fresh cilantro
2 garlic cloves, minced
2 tablespoons corn oil
2 tablespoons rice vinegar
1 tablespoon sesame oil
1 tablespoon lime juice
1 teaspoon red bell pepper flakes
1/4 teaspoon salt
1/4 teaspoon ginger

Place the corn and water in a saucepan. Bring to a boil. Reduce the heat to low. Simmer, covered, for 7 to 8 minutes or just until tender; drain.

Combine the corn, beans, cucumbers, chopped bell pepper, green onions, cilantro and garlic in a large bowl and mix well.

Whisk the corn oil, vinegar, sesame oil, lime juice, bell pepper flakes, salt and ginger in a small bowl until well mixed. Pour over the corn mixture. Refrigerate, covered, for at least 2 hours.

Yield: 12 servings

RICE ORIENTAL

1 tablespoon butter
1/3 cup finely chopped onion
1 cup rice
1/4 cup blanched almonds
2 teaspoons raisins
1 1/2 cups chicken broth
Salt and pepper to taste

Melt the butter in a saucepan. Add the onion. Cook until tender. Stir in the rice, almonds and raisins. Add the broth, salt and pepper. Bring to a boil. Reduce the heat to low. Simmer, covered, for 20 minutes or until the rice is tender and the broth is absorbed.

CARIBBEAN COCONUT CREAM PIE

3/4   cup sugar

3   tablespoons cornstarch

2   cups milk

3   egg yolks

2   tablespoons butter

1   teaspoon vanilla extract

1   cup flaked coconut

1   baked (9-inch) pie shell

3   egg whites

6   tablespoons sugar

Combine 3/4 cup sugar and cornstarch in a saucepan. Stir in the milk gradually. Cook until the mixture begins to boil, stirring constantly. Cook for 2 minutes, stirring constantly. Remove from the heat.

Place the egg yolks in a small bowl. Stir a small amount of the hot milk mixture into the egg yolks. Pour the egg yolk mixture gradually into the saucepan, stirring constantly. Cook for 2 minutes or until the mixture just coats a metal spoon, stirring constantly. Remove from the heat. Stir in the butter, vanilla and coconut. Pour into the pie shell.

Beat the egg whites in a large mixing bowl until soft peaks form. Add the 6 tablespoons sugar, 1 tablespoon at a time, beating until stiff peaks form. Spread the meringue over the top of the pie, sealing to the edge.

Bake at 350 degrees for 12 to 15 minutes. Let stand until cool.

Yield: 6 servings

POPPY SEED CAKE

1   (2-layer) package yellow cake mix
1   (3-ounce) package vanilla instant pudding mix
1   cup sour cream
4   eggs
1/2 cup vegetable oil
1/2 cup cream sherry
1/2 cup poppy seeds

Beat the cake mix, pudding mix, sour cream, eggs, oil, sherry and poppy seeds in a mixing bowl for 5 minutes. Pour into a greased and floured bundt or tube pan.

Bake at 350 degrees for 1 hour or until the cake tests done. Cool in the pan for 15 minutes. Invert onto a serving plate.

Yield: 16 servings

SEAFOAM COOKIES

2   cups sugar
1/2 cup water
1/2 cup light corn syrup
    Dash of salt
2   egg whites
    Chopped pecans or walnuts (optional)

Combine the sugar, water, corn syrup and salt in a saucepan and mix well. Cook, covered, until the mixture boils. Uncover the pan. Cook to 250 to 266 degrees on a candy thermometer, hard-ball stage.

Beat the egg whites in a mixing bowl until stiff peaks form. Pour the hot syrup over the egg whites. Beat until the mixture can be dropped from a spoon. Stir in the chopped nuts. Drop by teaspoonfuls onto waxed paper.

Yield: about 4 dozen

New Bern was—and still is—a great place to grow up! Gene McSorley, speaking in *An Oral History of New Bern,* describes the Coastguardsmen of the *Pamilico,* the cutter docked right next to Meadows Shipyard: "I don't know why they didn't treat us affectionately, but we seemed to upset them a little. If the wind was blowing the wrong way and we decided that we didn't want to paddle our homemade rafts anymore, we just waited for them to come get us."

From the Family Garden

Appetizers
Dip for Raw Vegetables
Dill Vegetable Dip

Soup
Broccoli Cheese Soup

Salads
Broccoli Salad
Grilled Vegetable Salad
Sesame Coleslaw

Main Dishes
Mustard Herb Chicken
Diane's Nutty Chicken
Penne with Tomatoes, Olives and Two Cheeses
Spinach Lasagna

Side Dishes
Microwave Bread and Butter Pickles
Watermelon Rind Pickles
Green Tomato Relish
Stewed Tomatoes, Squash and Onions
Grilled Summer Vegetables

Desserts
Carrot Cake • Blueberry Pie
Strawberry Rhubarb Pie
Zany Zucchini Bars

DIP FOR RAW VEGETABLES

8   ounces cream cheese, softened
1/3 cup milk
1/3 cup mayonnaise
2   tablespoons ketchup
2   tablespoons chopped green onions
1   tablespoon Worcestershire sauce
    Assorted fresh vegetables, cut into bite-size pieces
    (such as carrots, cauliflower, celery, mushrooms)

Beat the cream cheese and milk in a mixing bowl until smooth. Add the mayonnaise, ketchup, green onions and Worcestershire sauce and mix well. Refrigerate, covered, until ready to serve. Serve with assorted fresh vegetables for dipping.

Yield: 16 (2-tablespoon) servings

DILL VEGETABLE DIP

1   cup mayonnaise
1   cup sour cream
1   tablespoon dillweed
1   tablespoon seasoned salt
1   tablespoon parsley flakes
1   tablespoon minced onion
    Assorted fresh vegetables, cut up

Combine the mayonnaise, sour cream, dillweed, seasoned salt, parsley and onion in a bowl and mix well. Refrigerate, covered, for 8 hours or longer. Serve with assorted fresh vegetables for dipping.

Yield: 16 (2-tablespoon) servings

BROCCOLI CHEESE SOUP

2　to 3 cups chopped fresh broccoli
1/2　cup chopped carrots
1/4　cup chopped onion
1 1/2 cups chicken broth
1/2　teaspoon salt
2　tablespoons flour
1 1/2 cups milk
8　ounces Velveeta cheese

Combine the broccoli, carrots, onion, broth and salt in a saucepan. Bring to a boil. Reduce the heat to low. Simmer, covered, for 15 to 20 minutes or until the vegetables are tender.

Place the flour in a bowl. Add the milk gradually, stirring until blended. Stir the milk mixture into the vegetables. Cook until thickened. Add the cheese and stir until melted.

Yield: 6 to 8 servings

BROCCOLI SALAD

1　bunch broccoli, cut into florets
1　head cauliflower, cut into florets
1　small red onion, thinly sliced
1/2　cup chopped green bell pepper
1/2　cup thinly sliced carrots
1　cup shredded Cheddar cheese
1　pound bacon, crisp-cooked, crumbled
1　(2-ounce) package slivered almonds
　Broccoli Salad Dressing (at left)

Combine the florets, onion, bell pepper, carrots, cheese, bacon and almonds in a bowl. Add Broccoli Salad Dressing and toss to coat.

Yield: 10 servings

BROCCOLI SALAD
DRESSING

5　tablespoons vinegar
1　cup mayonnaise
1/4　cup sugar

Combine the vinegar, mayonnaise and sugar in a bowl and mix well. Refrigerate, covered, for 1 hour or longer.

GRILLED VEGETABLE SALAD

1/3 cup balsamic vinegar
2 tablespoons olive oil
2 shallots, finely chopped
1 1/2 teaspoons molasses
1 teaspoon Italian seasoning
1/4 teaspoon salt
1/4 teaspoon pepper
8 ounces carrots, cut into large chunks
1 red bell pepper, cut into large chunks
1 yellow or green bell pepper, cut into large chunks
2 zucchini, thickly sliced
2 yellow squash, thickly sliced
1 large onion, cut into large chunks

Combine the vinegar, olive oil, shallots, molasses, Italian seasoning, salt and pepper in a large bowl. Add the carrots, bell peppers, zucchini, yellow squash and onion to the vinegar mixture. Toss to coat. Let stand for 30 minutes, stirring occasionally.

Remove the vegetables from the vinegar mixture with a slotted spoon to a grill basket sprayed with nonstick cooking spray. Reserve the vinegar mixture.

Grill the vegetables over medium-hot coals for 15 to 20 minutes or until slightly charred, turning the basket occasionally.

Return the vegetables to the vinegar mixture in the bowl and toss. Serve warm or refrigerate, covered, and serve cold as a salad.

Note: You may also use mushrooms, snap beans or other vegetables.

Yield: 6 servings

SESAME COLESLAW

6   *cups very thinly sliced green cabbage*
3   *cups shredded carrots*
2   *cups fresh spinach leaves, trimmed, thinly sliced*
1/2   *cup plus 1 tablespoon rice vinegar*
1/4   *cup sesame oil*
1/4   *cup sugar*
3   *tablespoons minced gingerroot*
2   *teaspoons soy sauce*
     Salt and pepper to taste
     Additional fresh spinach leaves
1 1/2 *tablespoons sesame seeds, toasted*

Combine the cabbage, carrots and spinach in a bowl and mix well.

Whisk the vinegar, sesame oil, sugar, gingerroot and soy sauce in a small bowl until the sugar dissolves. Season the dressing with salt and pepper.

Add the dressing to the cabbage mixture and toss to mix. Season with salt and pepper. Line a serving platter with the spinach leaves. Mound the coleslaw in the center. Sprinkle with the sesame seeds.

Note: The cabbage mixture and dressing may be prepared up to 1 day in advance. Refrigerate, covered, in separate containers.

Yield: 12 servings

MUSTARD HERB CHICKEN

6   large boneless skinless chicken breast halves
    Mustard Herb Marinade (at right)

Place the chicken in a large shallow glass baking dish. Pour the Mustard Herb Marinade over the chicken. Marinate, covered, in the refrigerator for 4 hours; drain.

Discard the marinade. Grill the chicken about 5 inches from medium-hot coals for 10 minutes on each side or until cooked through. Arrange on a serving platter. Garnish with lemon slices and herb sprigs.

Yield: 6 servings

DIANE'S NUTTY CHICKEN

2   cups nonfat sour cream
1   tablespoon butter, melted
1   cup finely chopped hazelnuts, pecans or peanuts
6   boneless chicken breast halves
1   teaspoon (about) Dijon mustard

Combine 1/3 cup of the sour cream and the butter in a shallow dish and mix well. Place the hazelnuts in another shallow dish. Dip the chicken breasts in the sour cream mixture, then roll in the nuts to coat. Refrigerate, covered, for 3 hours. Place the chicken in a roasting pan. Bake at 350 degrees for 20 minutes or until cooked through. Remove the chicken to a platter and keep warm in a 200-degree oven.

Combine the remaining 1²/3 cups sour cream with enough mustard to produce a mild mustard flavor. Pour the drippings from the roasting pan and discard. Add the sour cream mixture to the pan and stir to scrape up any browned bits from the bottom. Spoon a portion of the sour cream mixture on each serving plate. Top with a warm chicken breast.

Yield: 6 servings

MUSTARD HERB
MARINADE

1/2 cup lemon juice
1/4 cup Dijon mustard
2   tablespoons finely chopped fresh basil
1   tablespoon finely chopped fresh parsley
1   tablespoon finely chopped fresh thyme
1   tablespoon vegetable oil
2   teaspoons grated lemon zest
    Salt and pepper to taste

Combine the lemon juice, mustard, basil, parsley, thyme, oil, lemon zest, salt and pepper in a bowl and mix well.

PENNE WITH TOMATOES, OLIVES AND TWO CHEESES

6   tablespoons olive oil
1 1/2 cups chopped onions
1   teaspoon minced garlic
3   (28-ounce) cans Italian plum tomatoes, drained
2   teaspoons dried basil
1 1/2 teaspoons crushed red pepper
2   cups low-sodium chicken broth
     Salt and black pepper to taste
1   pound uncooked penne or rigatoni
2 1/2 cups shredded Havarti cheese
1/3 cup sliced kalamata olives
1/3 cup grated Parmesan cheese
1/4 cup finely chopped fresh basil

Heat 3 tablespoons of the olive oil in a large heavy Dutch oven over medium-high heat. Add the onions and garlic. Sauté for 5 minutes or until the onions are tender. Stir in the tomatoes, dried basil and crushed red pepper. Bring to a boil, breaking up the tomatoes with the back of a spoon. Add the broth; return to a boil. Reduce the heat to medium. Simmer for 1 hour and 10 minutes or until the mixture thickens to a chunky sauce consistency and is reduced to 6 cups, stirring occasionally. Season with salt and black pepper.

Cook the penne in a large pot of boiling water until tender but firm to the bite (al dente). Drain well. Return the penne to the pot. Add the remaining 3 tablespoons olive oil, tossing to coat. Pour the tomato sauce over the pasta and toss to mix well. Stir in the Havarti cheese.

Spoon the pasta mixture into a 9×13-inch baking dish. Sprinkle with the olives and Parmesan cheese. Bake at 375 degrees for 30 minutes or until heated through. Sprinkle with the fresh basil.

Note: Sauce may be prepared up to 2 days ahead of time, covered and refrigerated. Reheat the sauce when ready to use.

Yield: 12 servings

SPINACH LASAGNA

1   (26-ounce) can spaghetti sauce
2/3 (10-ounce) package frozen chopped spinach, cooked, drained
15   ounces ricotta cheese
8   ounces lasagna noodles, cooked, drained
3   cups shredded mozzarella cheese

Heat the spaghetti sauce in a saucepan. Combine the spinach and ricotta cheese in a bowl and mix well.

Layer 3 noodles, 1/2 of the spinach mixture, 1/3 of the sauce and 1/3 of the mozzarella cheese in a 9×13-inch baking dish. Continue layering with 1/2 of the remaining noodles, the remaining spinach mixture, 1/2 of the remaining sauce and 1/2 of the remaining mozzarella cheese. Top with the remaining noodles, sauce and mozzarella cheese.

Bake at 350 degrees for 30 minutes or until heated through. Serve with grated Parmesan cheese.

Yield: 10 servings

Watermelon Rind Pickles

20 cups watermelon rind chunks
7   cups sugar
2   cups cider vinegar
1/4 teaspoon each ground cloves and cinnamon

Place the watermelon rind in a large pot with enough water to cover. Bring to a boil. Boil just until tender, but not mushy; drain. Combine the sugar, vinegar, cloves and cinnamon in a saucepan. Bring to a boil. Pour the hot syrup over the rind. Let stand for 8 hours or longer.

Drain the rind, reserving the syrup. Reheat the syrup in a saucepan to a boil. Pour over the rind and let stand again for 8 hours or longer. Repeat this process 2 more times. On the last day, reheat the rind and syrup in a pot. Spoon the rind mixture into hot sterilized jars, leaving 1/2 inch headspace; seal with 2-piece lids.

Yield: variable

Green Tomato Relish

8   quarts green tomatoes, finely chopped
12 medium onions, finely chopped
1/4 cup salt
4   cups cider vinegar
1   hot red chile, chopped (optional)
2   tablespoons each white mustard seeds and celery seeds
1   tablespoon turmeric

Combine the tomatoes, onions and salt in a pot. Add enough water to cover. Let stand, covered, for 8 hours or longer; drain. Stir in the remaining ingredients. Cook for 1 hour, adding more water if necessary. Pack the hot tomato mixture into hot sterilized jars, leaving 1/2 inch headspace; seal with 2-piece lids. Let stand for 5 weeks before serving.

Yield: variable

STEWED TOMATOES, SQUASH AND ONION

4   cups thinly sliced zucchini, pattypan or yellow squash
1   medium onion, chopped
2   tomatoes, peeled, chopped
1   sprig of fresh basil
2   tablespoons butter or margarine
    Salt and pepper to taste

Cook the zucchini and onion in a heavy nonstick saucepan for 5 minutes. Add the tomatoes and basil. Simmer, covered, for 15 minutes or until the zucchini is tender, stirring once or twice. Stir in the butter, salt and pepper.

Yield: 4 servings

GRILLED SUMMER VEGETABLES

1   pound fresh baby carrots
1   red bell pepper, cut into 1-inch squares
1   yellow bell pepper, cut into 1-inch squares
2   zucchini, diagonally sliced
2   yellow squash, diagonally sliced
1   large red onion, cut into eighths
1   (8-ounce) bottle light olive oil vinaigrette

Marinate the carrots, bell peppers, zucchini, yellow squash and red onion in the vinaigrette in a bowl for 2 to 8 hours; drain. Place in a grill basket. Grill the vegetables over hot coals for 15 minutes or until tender and lightly charred but not limp.

Note: The vegetables may also be broiled in the oven on a foil-lined baking sheet. Any leftovers are delicious served cold.

Yield: 16 servings

CARROT CAKE

Cake

1 1/2 cups vegetable oil
2 cups sugar
4 eggs
1 teaspoon baking soda
1 teaspoon cinnamon
2 cups self-rising flour
2 cups shredded carrots

Cream Cheese Frosting

1/2 cup (1 stick) butter, softened
8 ounces cream cheese, softened
1 (1-pound) package confectioners' sugar
1 cup chopped pecans

For the cake, beat the oil and sugar in a mixing bowl. Add the eggs 1 at a time, beating well after each addition. Beat in the baking soda and cinnamon. Add the flour gradually and mix well. Stir in the carrots. Pour into 2 greased and floured 9-inch round cake pans.

Bake at 350 degrees for 32 to 35 minutes or until the cake tests done. Cool in the pans for 10 minutes. Remove to wire racks to cool completely.

For the frosting, beat the butter and cream cheese in a mixing bowl until light and fluffy. Beat in the confectioners' sugar. Stir in the pecans.

Spread the frosting between the layers and over the top and side of the cooled cake.

Yield: 12 servings

BLUEBERRY PIE

2/3   cup sugar
5   teaspoons flour
1/4   teaspoon cinnamon
4   cups fresh blueberries
1   (2-crust) pie pastry
1   tablespoon butter

Combine the sugar, flour and cinnamon in a bowl and mix well. Fold in the blueberries. Pour into a pastry-lined pie plate. Dot with the butter. Top with the remaining pastry, fluting the edge to form a high rim and cutting vents.

Bake at 425 degrees for 35 to 40 minutes or until golden brown. Serve with vanilla ice cream if desired.

Yield: 6 servings

STRAWBERRY RHUBARB PIE

3   cups sliced strawberries
3   cups sliced rhubarb
2   cups sugar
1/4   cup flour
2   tablespoons tapioca
1/4   teaspoon cinnamon
1   (2-crust) pie pastry
2   tablespoons butter

Combine the strawberries and rhubarb in a bowl and mix well. Add the sugar, flour, tapioca and cinnamon and mix well. Pour into a pastry-lined pie plate. Dot with the butter. Top with the remaining pastry, sealing the edge and cutting vents. Bake at 350 degrees for 45 minutes.

Yield: 6 servings

ZANY ZUCCHINI BARS

2	cups sugar
4	eggs
1 1/2	cups vegetable oil
2	cups shredded zucchini
2	cups flour
2	teaspoons baking soda
2	teaspoons cinnamon
3/4	teaspoon salt
1/2	cup chopped nuts (optional)
1/4	cup (1/2 stick) butter, softened
6	ounces cream cheese, softened
3 1/2	cups confectioners' sugar
4	teaspoons vanilla extract

Beat the sugar and eggs in a mixing bowl. Add the oil and zucchini and mix well. Stir in the flour, baking soda, cinnamon, salt and nuts. Pour into a greased 10×15-inch baking pan.

Bake at 350 degrees for 20 to 25 minutes or until the layer tests done. Cool in the pan.

Cream the butter, cream cheese, confectioners' sugar and vanilla in a mixing bowl until light and fluffy. Frost the cooled layer. Cut into bars.

Yield: 36 servings

AUTUMN

DURING
THE *A*UTUMN
MONTHS

Younger family members gathered around the kitchen table to wonder at the autumn's harvest...abundant squash, pumpkins, and collard greens in whose growth these young farmers had played a part. Farther afield, even today, "King Cotton" ripens and deepens to a snowy white against the clear blue October sky. Following in the tradition of his antebellum ancestors who hosted hunting parties at their plantations, today's hunter still stalks the woods and returns with deer and pheasant for an evening meal.

Weyerhaeuser Real Estate Company

$\mathcal{A}$FTER THE $\mathcal{H}$UNT

PAGE 109

$\mathcal{C}$ELEBRATING $\mathcal{M}$UMS AND $\mathcal{G}$HOSTS

PAGE 124

$\mathcal{C}$ELEBRATING THE $\mathcal{H}$ARVEST

PAGE 136

$\mathcal{H}$OMECOMING $\mathcal{T}$AILGATE

PAGE 148

CELEBRATING THE HARVEST

After the Hunt

Soup
Down East Clam Chowder

Salad
Duck and Walnut Salad

Main Dishes
Venison Ham
All-Day Deer Roast
Venison Medallions with Creamy Mushroom Sauce
Hunter's Stew
Cornish Hens with Currant Sauce
Dove Pie
Shrimp au Gratin
Pheasant with Scotch Whiskey
Scalloped Oysters

Side Dishes
Wild Game Sauce
Phillips' Filthy Rice
Herb-Roasted Potatoes Poupon

Bread
Irish Soda Bread

Desserts
Orange Raisin Cake
Apple Crumb Pie
Sinful Chocolate Pie

DOWN EAST CLAM CHOWDER

2   to 4 slices bacon, chopped
2   large onions, chopped
2   (32-ounce) bags frozen southern-style hash brown potatoes
8   (6-ounce) cans chopped clams in clam juice
1   to 2 tablespoons chopped parsley, dried or fresh
1   tablespoon Worcestershire sauce
    Salt and pepper to taste
    Tabasco sauce or Texas Pete hot sauce to taste

Cook the bacon in a large saucepan until lightly browned. Add the onions. Cook until softened and lightly browned. Stir in the potatoes, undrained clams, parsley, Worcestershire sauce, salt, pepper and Tabasco sauce. Add enough water to cover all the ingredients. Bring to a boil. Reduce the heat to low. Simmer, covered, for 45 minutes to 1 hour or until the desired consistency is reached.

Yield: 12 servings

DUCK AND WALNUT SALAD

2 duck breast fillets
  Salt and pepper to taste
1/2 cup walnut halves
2 tablespoons raspberry vinegar
1/4 cup walnut oil
2 tablespoons peanut oil
1 tablespoon sugar
2 teaspoons soy sauce
1 head romaine lettuce, cut into bite-size pieces
1 cucumber, peeled, thinly sliced
2 tablespoons chopped green onions

Season the duck breasts with salt and pepper. Place on a rack in a roasting pan. Roast at 350 degrees for 40 minutes. Cool and thinly slice.

Spread the walnuts on a baking sheet. Bake at 350 degrees for 10 to 15 minutes or until browned, stirring several times during baking.

Whisk the vinegar, walnut oil, peanut oil, sugar and soy sauce in a small bowl until blended. Combine the lettuce and cucumber in a large bowl. Add half the dressing mixture and toss to coat. Divide the lettuce and cucumber among 4 salad bowls. Top each with equal amounts of sliced duck. Spoon the remaining dressing over the duck. Garnish with the toasted walnuts and green onions.

Yield: 4 servings

Venison Ham

4 quarts water
1 1/2 quarts vinegar
3 large onions, chopped
2 carrots, diced
1 garlic clove, chopped
3 tablespoons salt
2 teaspoons thyme
10 sprigs of parsley
20 to 30 peppercorns
3 dashes of Worcestershire sauce
3 dashes of Tabasco sauce
1 deer ham
  Chopped garlic
  Salt, ground pepper, seasoned salt and garlic salt to taste
  Salt pork, sliced
  Worcestershire sauce to taste
  Vegetable oil

Combine the water, vinegar, onions, carrots, 1 garlic clove, 3 tablespoons salt, thyme, parsley, peppercorns, 3 dashes of Worcestershire sauce and Tabasco sauce in a large saucepan. Bring to a boil. Reduce the heat to low. Simmer, covered, for 1 hour. Cool for 30 minutes to 1 hour.

Place the deer ham in a roasting pan. Cover with garlic. Season with salt and ground pepper to taste. Pour the cooled vinegar mixture over the ham. Marinate, covered, in the refrigerator for 24 to 48 hours, turning once; drain.

Remove the fat and tough sinews from the ham. Sprinkle both sides with seasoned salt and garlic salt. Cover the top with salt pork slices. Season with Worcestershire sauce to taste.

Place the roasting pan in a 450-degree oven for 3 to 5 minutes. Remove from the oven. Place the ham in the hot pan. Add enough oil to cover the bottom of the pan. Roast for about 1 1/2 hours, basting with the oil.

Yield: Variable

ALL-DAY DEER ROAST

1   (6- to 8-pound) deer ham or (5-pound) neck roast
6   to 8 slices bacon
2   large onions, sliced
    Pepper to taste
    Seasoned salt to taste
1   bay leaf
    Worcestershire sauce to taste

Pierce the ham end to end with a large knife. Stuff each hole with a bacon slice, using the handle of a wooden spoon.

Cover the bottom of a slow cooker with half the onions. Place the ham over the onions. Top with the remaining onions. Season with pepper and seasoned salt. Add the bay leaf. Drizzle Worcestershire sauce liberally over the top. Cook on Low for 6 to 8 hours. Remove and discard the bay leaf.

Yield: Variable

VENISON MEDALLIONS WITH CREAMY MUSHROOM SAUCE

2   tablespoons butter
2   tablespoons flour
1/2   cup chicken broth
1/4   cup white wine
1/4   cup heavy cream
1   teaspoon Worcestershire sauce
     Dash of Tabasco sauce (optional)
2   cups sliced fresh mushrooms
1/2   cup diced green bell pepper
1/2   cup diced red bell pepper
2   green onions, diced
2   garlic cloves, minced
12   (3-ounce) venison medallions (1/2 to 1/3 inch thick)
     Salt and pepper to taste
2   tablespoons olive oil

Melt the butter in a saucepan over medium heat. Whisk in the flour gradually. Cook for 4 to 5 minutes or until the mixture is smooth and light brown, stirring constantly. Whisk in the broth gradually. Stir in the wine and cream until well blended. Add the Worcestershire sauce, Tabasco sauce, mushrooms, bell peppers, green onions and garlic. Simmer for 10 to 12 minutes, stirring frequently.

Season the venison medallions with salt and pepper. Heat the olive oil in a skillet over medium-high heat. Add the medallions. Cook on both sides until medium-rare or done to taste.

Spoon the mushroom sauce onto a serving plate. Arrange the medallions over the sauce.

Yield: 4 servings

HUNTER'S STEW

2   tablespoons vegetable oil
1 1/2 pounds boneless venison, cut into 1/2-inch cubes
8   ounces smoked sausage, cut into 1/2-inch slices
1/2 cup each chopped onion and chopped celery
2   (28-ounce) cans chopped tomatoes
1   (12-ounce) can beer
1   teaspoon each salt and sugar
1/2 teaspoon rosemary, crushed
1/2 teaspoon each basil and freshly ground pepper
2   carrots, diced
2   medium potatoes, cut into cubes

Heat the oil in a Dutch oven. Add the venison and sausage. Cook until browned. Add the onion and celery. Cook until the vegetables are tender.

Stir in the undrained tomatoes, beer, salt, sugar, rosemary, basil and pepper. Bring to a boil. Reduce the heat to low. Simmer, covered, for 30 minutes.

Stir in the carrots. Cook, uncovered, for 30 minutes. Add the potatoes. Cook for 30 minutes or until tender.

Yield: 10 servings

CORNISH HENS WITH CURRANT SAUCE

Currant Sauce (at right)
2   large Cornish game hens

Brush some of the Currant Sauce over the surface of the game hens. Place in a roasting pan or Dutch oven. Bake, covered, at 350 degrees for 1 hour, basting every 15 minutes with the remaining sauce. Bake, uncovered, for 15 minutes or until cooked through. Cut the game hens into halves. Serve with brown rice topped with the pan juices.

Yield: 4 servings

CURRANT SAUCE

1/4 cup (1/2 stick) butter or margarine
1/2 cup sherry
1/2 (12-ounce) jar currant jelly
     Juice of 1 lemon
1   tablespoon salt
1   teaspoon dry mustard
1   teaspoon paprika

Melt the butter in a saucepan. Add the sherry. Bring to a boil. Stir in the jelly, lemon juice, salt, dry mustard and paprika. Boil for 5 minutes. Cool.

DOVE PIE

8   to 12 dove breasts
1   cup heavy cream
1   (10-ounce) can cream of chicken soup
    Pepper to taste
1   (2-crust) pie pastry

Combine the dove breasts with enough water to cover in a saucepan. Bring to a boil. Cook until the dove is cooked through; drain. Let cool. Remove the dove from the bones and cut into bite-size pieces.

Distribute the dove evenly over the bottom of a 1¹/₂-quart round baking dish. Top with a mixture of the cream and soup. Season with pepper.

Roll the pastry into a circle slightly larger than the diameter of the baking dish on a lightly floured surface. Place over the baking dish, sealing the edge and cutting vents. Bake at 375 degrees for 30 to 35 minutes or until the crust is brown.

Note: You may substitute any small game (rabbit, squirrel, quail, duck) for the dove. For a more traditional crust, top the pie with biscuit dough, rolled thinly.

Yield: 6 servings

SHRIMP AU GRATIN

2 1/2 quarts water
3   pounds fresh unpeeled medium shrimp
1/3 cup butter or margarine
1/2 cup flour
1   cup chicken broth
1   cup heavy cream
1   cup shredded Swiss cheese
2   tablespoons plus 1 1/2 teaspoons dry sherry
1   teaspoon Worcestershire sauce
1/4 teaspoon salt
1/8 teaspoon white pepper
1/8 teaspoon hot red pepper sauce
3   tablespoons grated Parmesan cheese
     Hot cooked angel hair pasta

Bring the water to a boil in a saucepan. Add the shrimp. Cook for 3 to 5 minutes or until the shrimp turn pink; drain. Rinse with cold water. Refrigerate, covered, until chilled. Peel and devein the shrimp; set aside.

Melt the butter in a heavy saucepan over low heat. Add the flour, stirring until smooth. Cook for 1 minute, stirring constantly. Stir in the broth and cream gradually. Cook over medium heat until thickened and bubbly, stirring constantly. Add the Swiss cheese, sherry, Worcestershire sauce, salt, white pepper and pepper sauce, stirring until the cheese melts. Stir in the shrimp. Spoon into a lightly greased 2-quart baking dish. Sprinkle with the Parmesan cheese.

Bake at 350 degrees for 40 minutes or until heated through and bubbly. Serve over hot pasta.

Note: You may prepare ahead of time. Prepare shrimp mixture as directed, but do not bake. Refrigerate, covered, for up to 8 hours. Remove from the refrigerator 30 minutes before baking. Uncover and bake as directed.

Yield: 6 servings

$\mathcal{P}$HEASANT WITH SCOTCH WHISKEY

1   *pheasant, cut into quarters*
Salt and pepper to taste
1/4 *cup (1/2 stick) butter or vegetable oil*
1/2 *cup chicken broth*
1/2 *cup Scotch whiskey*

Season the pheasant with salt and pepper. Melt the butter in a skillet over low heat. Add the pheasant. Increase the heat to medium-high. Sauté until golden brown on all sides, turning frequently.

Line a small roaster, or other ovenproof pan with a lid, with foil. Remove the pheasant to the pan. Add enough water to cover half the bird. Add the broth and Scotch. Cover the pan tightly with foil and the lid. Bake at 350 degrees for about 3 hours or until very tender. Serve with wild rice.

Note: If a stronger whiskey flavor is desired, add the Scotch to the pan after baking for 30 minutes. The pan juices make a wonderful gravy.

Yield: 4 servings

SCALLOPED OYSTERS

2 1/2 cups finely chopped onions
2 1/2 cups finely chopped celery
1 cup (2 sticks) butter
1 (13-ounce) package oyster crackers
2 pints oysters, rinsed
2 cups half-and-half

Sauté the onions and celery in a small amount of the butter in a skillet; set aside.

Melt 1/2 cup of the butter in a saucepan. Remove from the heat. Add the oyster crackers and toss to mix.

Layer 1/2 of the crackers, the onion mixture and the oysters in a buttered 1 1/2-quart baking dish. Top with the remaining crackers. Dot with the remaining butter. Pour in the half-and-half.

Bake at 350 degrees for about 1 hour.

Yield: 6 servings

PHILLIPS' FILTHY RICE

1 pound bulk pork sausage
1 (4-ounce) can mushrooms
1 (15-ounce) can kidney beans
1 tablespoon crushed red pepper
1 (6-ounce) package brown and wild rice mix

Brown the sausage in a skillet, stirring until crumbly; drain.

Combine the sausage, mushrooms, beans, crushed red pepper and rice mix in a large saucepan. Cook according to the rice mix package directions.

Yield: 4 servings

WILD GAME SAUCE

1 cup vinegar
1 cup mustard
1 cup molasses
1/4 cup Worcestershire sauce
2 bay leaves
1 teaspoon sweet pickle cubes
1 teaspoon Italian seasoning
1/2 teaspoon garlic salt
1/2 teaspoon seasoned salt
20 peppercorns
1/2 teaspoon ground black pepper

Combine the vinegar, mustard and molasses in a saucepan. Add the remaining ingredients and mix well. Bring to a boil. Serve with dove, duck, venison and other game.

HERB-ROASTED POTATOES POUPON

1/3   *cup Grey Poupon Dijon mustard*
2   *tablespoons olive oil*
1   *garlic clove, minced*
1/2   *teaspoon Italian seasoning*
      Chopped fresh rosemary to taste
6   *medium red-skinned potatoes (about 2 pounds), cut into chunks*

Combine the mustard, olive oil, garlic, Italian seasoning and rosemary in a small bowl and mix well. Place the potatoes in a lightly greased 9×13-inch baking dish or on a baking sheet. Pour the mustard mixture over and toss to coat.

Bake at 425 degrees for 35 to 40 minutes or until the potatoes are tender.

Note: For an easier way to coat the potatoes, place them in a sealable plastic bag. Add the mustard mixture, seal and shake. Potatoes may also be placed in a foil pan and cooked on the grill.

Yield: 4 servings

IRISH SODA BREAD

4 1/2 cups flour
3   tablespoons sugar
1   tablespoon baking powder
1   teaspoon salt
1   teaspoon baking soda
6   tablespoons butter
2   eggs
1 1/2 cups buttermilk

Combine the flour, sugar, baking powder, salt and baking soda in a bowl and mix well. Cut in the butter until crumbly. Beat the eggs in a bowl. Remove 1 tablespoon of the beaten egg and set aside. Combine the buttermilk with the remaining eggs. Stir into the flour mixture to form a dough.

Knead the dough on a floured surface 10 times. Shape into a ball. Place on a greased baking sheet. Cut a cross in the top of the dough with a sharp knife. Brush with the reserved beaten egg.

Bake at 350 degrees for 1 hour and 10 minutes. Remove to a wire rack to cool.

Note: You may add 1 1/2 cups raisins and/or 1 tablespoon caraway seeds to the flour mixture. If adding the raisins, decrease the flour to 4 cups.

Yield: 12 servings

Although we think of the fall months as the Harvest time, summer boasts bountiful harvests from the sea and the smaller tributaries leading to it—marlin, tuna, mahi-mahi (dolphin), tarpon, mussels, and clams. And, of course, shrimp and crabs are served up in boils, roasted over hot coals, or marinated and grilled.

ORANGE RAISIN CAKE

Cake

1	orange
1	cup raisins
1/2	cup (1 stick) margarine, softened
1	cup sugar
2	eggs
2	cups flour
1	teaspoon baking powder
1	teaspoon baking soda
1/4	teaspoon salt
1	cup buttermilk
1	teaspoon black walnut flavoring

Coconut Topping

1	cup packed brown sugar
1	cup evaporated milk
1	cup flaked coconut
1/4	cup (1/2 stick) margarine, melted

For the cake, cut the unpeeled orange into chunks. Grind the orange with the raisins in a blender or food processor; set aside.

Cream the 1/2 cup margarine and sugar in a mixing bowl until light and fluffy. Beat in the eggs.

Combine the flour, baking powder, baking soda and salt in a bowl. Add to the creamed mixture alternately with the buttermilk, mixing well after each addition. Stir in the orange mixture and flavoring. Pour into a greased 9×13-inch baking pan.

Bake at 350 degrees for 35 minutes or until the cake tests done.

For the topping, combine the brown sugar, evaporated milk, coconut and 1/4 cup margarine in a bowl and mix well. Pour over the hot baked cake. Broil until the topping is bubbly. Cool on a wire rack.

Yield: 15 servings

Apple Crumb Pie

4   to 6 cooking apples, peeled, sliced
1   unbaked (9-inch) deep-dish pie shell
1/2 cup sugar
1   tablespoon cornstarch
1   teaspoon apple pie spice
    Crumb Topping (at right)

Place the apples in the pie shell. Combine the sugar, cornstarch and apple pie spice in a bowl and mix well. Sprinkle over the apples. Sprinkle the Crumb Topping over the top. Bake on the lowest oven rack at 400 degrees for 45 minutes to 1 hour or until the apples are tender and the topping is browned. Cool on a wire rack for 1 to 2 hours before serving.

Yield: 6 servings

CRUMB TOPPING

1/2 cup sugar
1/3 cup butter, softened
1/2 cup flour

Combine the sugar, butter and flour in a bowl and mix until crumbly.

Sinful Chocolate Pie

2   (4-ounce) packages German's sweet chocolate, broken into squares
1/4 cup milk
8   ounces cream cheese, softened
2   tablespoons sugar
1/4 cup milk
8   ounces whipped topping
1   (9-inch) chocolate crumb pie shell

Reserve 3 squares of the chocolate. Place the remaining chocolate and 1/4 cup milk in a large microwave-safe bowl. Microwave on High for 1 to 2 minutes or until the chocolate is melted, stirring once. Beat in the cream cheese, sugar and 1/4 cup milk. Stir in the whipped topping gently until the mixture is smooth. Spoon into the pie shell. Freeze, covered, until firm. Remove the pie from the freezer 30 minutes before serving. Microwave the remaining 3 squares of chocolate in a microwave-safe bowl for 15 seconds or until melted. Drizzle over the pie.

Yield: 6 servings

CELEBRATING MUMS AND GHOSTS

BEVERAGE
Tropicana Punch

APPETIZERS
Tasty Chicken Wings
Beer Batter Shrimp
Feta Cheese Bites

SOUP
Tomato Herb Soup

MAIN DISHES
McStroganoff
Georgia Bird's Spaghetti Sauce
Saucy Pork Chops
Chicken Fiesta
Honey Ginger Salmon

SIDE DISHES
German Potato Salad
Dumplings with Sauerkraut
Vegetable Pudding

DESSERTS
Applesauce Cake
Pumpkin Pie
Pecan Tasties

TROPICANA PUNCH

2 (12-ounce) cans Tropicana frozen orange-strawberry or
   peach juice concentrate, thawed
1 (2-liter) bottle ginger ale
   Ice
   Fruit slices (such as oranges, strawberries)

Combine the juice concentrate and ginger ale in a punch bowl. Stir in ice.
Garnish with fruit slices.

Yield: about 20 servings

TASTY CHICKEN WINGS

1   (8-ounce) can crushed pineapple in juice
1   cup soy sauce
1/2 to 1 cup packed brown sugar
2   to 4 tablespoons mustard
24 chicken drumettes
1   (15-ounce) can baby corn, drained (optional)

Drain the pineapple, reserving the juice. Add enough water to the juice to
measure 1/2 cup. Combine the juice mixture, soy sauce, brown sugar and
mustard in a saucepan. Heat until the sugar dissolves, stirring occasionally.

Place the chicken drumettes in a baking dish. Arrange the corn over the
drumettes. Top with the crushed pineapple. Pour in the soy sauce mixture.
Bake at 250 degrees for 4 hours.

Yield: 6 to 8 servings

BEER BATTER SHRIMP

1/2 cup flour
1/2 cup cornmeal
1 (12-ounce) can beer
1 cup flour
1 tablespoon salt
1 tablespoon paprika
1 pound fresh deveined peeled shrimp
  Vegetable oil for frying

Mix 1/2 cup flour and cornmeal in a shallow bowl. Combine the beer, 1 cup flour, salt and paprika in a separate bowl and mix to form a batter.

Pat the shrimp dry. Dredge in the flour mixture. Dip in the batter. Deep-fry, a few at a time, in 375-degree oil for 2 to 3 minutes or until golden brown and cooked through. Drain on paper towels.

Yield: 3 servings

FETA CHEESE BITES

2 cups baking mix
1 cup plain yogurt
1 egg, beaten
1 tablespoon parsley flakes
1 teaspoon dillweed
1/4 to 1/2 cup milk
8 ounces feta cheese, drained, crumbled

Mix the baking mix, yogurt, egg, parsley and dillweed in a bowl. Stir in enough of the milk to make a stiff batter. Spread evenly in a greased 9×13-inch baking dish. Press the feta cheese into the top of the batter.

Bake at 350 degrees for 30 to 40 minutes or until the crust is golden brown.

Yield: 8 servings

TOMATO HERB SOUP

1   large onion, chopped
1/2 cup (1 stick) butter
1/2 cup flour
2   cups milk
2   cups chicken stock
1/3 cup chopped fresh parsley
1/3 cup dried basil
2   (16-ounce) cans tomatoes
1   (46-ounce) can tomato juice
   Salt and pepper to taste
   Grated Parmesan cheese

Sauté the onion in the butter in a saucepan. Add the flour, stirring constantly. Cook briefly. Add the milk and stock gradually, stirring constantly. Stir in the parsley and basil.

Combine the onion mixture, undrained tomatoes and tomato juice in a large stockpot and mix well. Bring to a boil. Season with salt and pepper. Serve immediately garnished with Parmesan cheese.

Yield: 12 servings

McStroganoff

New Bern at Night (the annual Ghost Walk, sponsored by the New Bern Historical Society) brings New Bern's ghosts to life on a tour through historic homes and along the streets of downtown New Bern—at night, of course. Cedar Grove Cemetery is always the scariest of haunts!

1	pound round steak, cut into cubes or strips
	Flour for dredging
1 1/2	tablespoons vegetable oil
1	cup sliced fresh mushrooms, or 1 (6-ounce) can sliced mushrooms, drained
1/2	cup chopped onion
1	garlic clove, minced
1	cup sour cream
1	(10-ounce) can tomato soup
6	to 8 drops of Tabasco sauce
1/2	teaspoon salt
	Dash of freshly ground pepper
1	cup rice, cooked, or 1 (8-ounce) package spaghetti, cooked
	Grated Parmesan cheese

Dredge the steak in flour to coat. Heat the oil in a large ovenproof skillet over medium-high heat. Brown the steak with the mushrooms, onion and garlic in the hot oil. Remove from the heat.

Combine the sour cream, soup, Tabasco sauce, salt and pepper in a bowl and mix well. Pour over the steak and vegetables. Bake, covered, at 350 degrees for 1 hour or until the steak is tender, stirring occasionally.

Serve over hot cooked rice or spaghetti. Sprinkle with Parmesan cheese.

Note: You may cook on top of the stove; simmer over low heat, stirring often to prevent sticking.

Yield: 4 servings

GEORGIA BIRD'S SPAGHETTI SAUCE

1   large yellow onion, chopped
4   celery ribs, chopped
1   green bell pepper, chopped
4   garlic cloves, minced
1   tablespoon extra-virgin olive oil
1 1/2 pounds ground beef
    Salt and pepper to taste
1   (4-ounce) can mushroom stems and pieces, drained
3   (6-ounce) cans tomato paste
1   tablespoon sugar
1   tablespoon oregano
2 1/4 to 3 cups water

Sauté the onion, celery, bell pepper and garlic in the olive oil in a large saucepan until tender. Add the ground beef. Cook until brown and crumbly; drain. Season with salt and pepper.

Stir in the mushrooms, tomato paste, sugar, oregano and enough water to make of the desired consistency. Bring to a boil. Reduce the heat to low. Simmer, covered, for 5 hours or longer.

Note: This sauce freezes well.

Yield: 8 to 10 servings

CHICKEN FIESTA

SAUCY PORK CHOPS

6   pork chops
1   tablespoon
    vegetable oil
1   (10-ounce) can
    cream of chicken
    soup
2   tablespoons
    Worcestershire
    sauce
1   cup ketchup
    Salt and pepper
    to taste
1   large onion, sliced

Brown the pork chops
in the oil in a skillet.
Combine the soup,
Worcestershire sauce,
ketchup, salt and
pepper in a bowl and
mix well. Pour over the
browned chops. Top
with the onion. Simmer
for 45 minutes to 1
hour or until the pork
chops are tender and
cooked through. Serve
with hot cooked rice.

1/4   cup (1/2 stick) butter
1/2   cup flour
2   eggs, beaten
6   boneless skinless chicken breast halves, pounded 1/2 inch thick
1   teaspoon butter
2   teaspoons flour
1/4   cup white wine
     Juice of 2 limes
11/2 cups chicken broth
2   teaspoons minced fresh cilantro
1/2   teaspoon salt
1/4   teaspoon pepper

Melt 1/4 cup butter in a large skillet. Place 1/2 cup flour and eggs in 2 separate shallow dishes. Coat the chicken in the flour, then dip in the beaten eggs. Add to the skillet. Sauté until golden brown on both sides. Remove the chicken from the skillet; set aside.

Melt 1 teaspoon butter in the same skillet over low heat. Stir in 2 teaspoons flour to make a smooth paste. Whisk in the wine gradually. Add the lime juice, broth, cilantro, salt and pepper, whisking constantly.

Return the chicken to the skillet. Simmer gently for 10 to 15 minutes or until the chicken is cooked through.

Yield: 6 servings

HONEY GINGER SALMON

6 tablespoons honey
1/4 cup chopped fresh cilantro
1/4 cup hoisin sauce
1 1/2 tablespoons minced gingerroot
1 tablespoon each canned chopped green chiles and brown sugar
4 (8-ounce) salmon steaks
Vegetable oil
Salt and pepper to taste

Combine the honey, cilantro, hoisin sauce, gingerroot, chiles and brown sugar in a bowl and mix well.

Brush the salmon steaks with oil. Season with salt and pepper. Brush some of the honey ginger glaze over the salmon. Place on a rack in a broiler pan. Broil for 4 minutes on each side or until the salmon flakes easily, basting occasionally with the remaining glaze.

Yield: 4 servings

GERMAN POTATO SALAD

8 ounces bacon, diced
1 medium onion, chopped
2 cups water
1 cup vinegar
1 1/2 cups sugar
1/2 cup flour
12 medium potatoes, cooked, peeled, cubed
Salt and pepper to taste

Cook the bacon in a skillet until crisp. Pour off half the drippings from the skillet. Add the onion. Cook until tender but not browned. Stir in the water, vinegar, sugar and flour. Cook until thickened, stirring constantly. Pour over the potatoes in a bowl and toss to mix. Season with salt and pepper.

Yield: 6 to 8 servings

DUMPLINGS WITH SAUERKRAUT

1   (32-ounce) container sauerkraut
1 1/2 cups sifted flour
1   tablespoon baking powder
1/4 teaspoon salt
1   egg, beaten
1/4 cup milk

Heat the sauerkraut in a saucepan until boiling. Sift the flour, baking powder and salt into a bowl. Add the egg, stirring with a fork. Stir in the milk and mix well. Drop by spoonfuls onto the boiling sauerkraut (not the liquid). Cover the pan tightly. Steam over low heat for 20 minutes without uncovering.

Yield: 8 servings

VEGETABLE PUDDING

1   medium winter squash, cooked, peeled
1/2 cup flour
1   cup sugar
2   eggs
1/4 cup (1/2 stick) butter or margarine
1/2 cup milk
1   teaspoon lemon flavoring
1   teaspoon nutmeg (optional)

Mash the squash in a large bowl. Add the flour, sugar, eggs, butter, milk, lemon flavoring and nutmeg and mix well. Spoon into a greased rectangular baking pan. Bake at 400 degrees for 20 to 25 minutes or until a wooden pick inserted in the center comes out clean.

Yield: 4 to 6 servings

APPLESAUCE CAKE

1   cup vegetable oil
2   cups sugar
2   cups Homemade Applesauce (at right)
1 1/2 teaspoons ground cloves
1 1/2 teaspoons nutmeg
1 1/2 teaspoons cinnamon
1/2 teaspoon salt
3   cups self-rising flour
1   cup raisins
1   cup chopped nuts

Beat the oil, sugar, Homemade Applesauce, cloves, nutmeg, cinnamon and salt in a mixing bowl until well blended. Stir in the flour 1 cup at a time. Add the raisins and nuts and mix well. Pour into a greased and floured tube pan.

Bake at 350 degrees for 1 1/2 hours or until the cake tests done. Cool in the pan for 10 minutes. Remove to a wire rack to cool completely.

Yield: 16 servings

HOMEMADE
APPLESAUCE

4   large Golden
       Delicious apples,
       peeled and diced
1   cup sugar
1/2 cup packed brown
       sugar

Place the apples in a saucepan. Add enough water to just cover the apples. Stir in the sugar and brown sugar. Bring to a boil. Cook until tender. Mash the apples. Cool completely.

PUMPKIN PIE

SPICED NUT CRUST

1   cup flour
1/2 cup finely chopped
    nuts
1/4 cup packed brown
    sugar
6   tablespoons butter,
    melted
1/2 teaspoon cinnamon
16 to 18 pecan halves

Combine the flour, chopped nuts, brown sugar, butter and cinnamon in a bowl and mix well. Press over the bottom and up the side of a 9-inch pie pan. Press the pecan halves onto the rim of the crust at 1-inch intervals.

1   (16-ounce) can pumpkin
1   (14-ounce) can sweetened condensed milk
2   eggs, beaten
1   teaspoon cinnamon
1/2 teaspoon ginger
1/2 teaspoon nutmeg
1/4 teaspoon salt
    Spiced Nut Crust (at left)

Combine the pumpkin, sweetened condensed milk, eggs, cinnamon, ginger, nutmeg and salt in a bowl and mix well. Pour into the Spiced Nut Crust.

Bake at 350 degrees for 50 to 55 minutes or until a knife inserted near the center comes out clean. Cool on a wire rack.

Yield: 6 servings

PECAN TASTIES

    1   cup (2 sticks) margarine, softened
    6   ounces cream cheese, softened
    2   cups flour
    2   eggs
    1¹/2 cups packed brown sugar
    2   tablespoons butter or margarine, melted
    1   teaspoon vanilla extract
    *   Pinch of salt*
    1   cup chopped pecans

Cream the margarine and cream cheese in a mixing bowl until light and fluffy. Blend in the flour to form a soft dough. Shape into a ball. Wrap in waxed paper. Refrigerate, covered, for 8 to 12 hours.

Combine the eggs, brown sugar, butter, vanilla and salt in a bowl and mix well.

Press 1 olive-size piece of chilled dough over the bottom and up the side of a greased miniature muffin cup using a pastry tamper or your fingers. Sprinkle some of the pecans over the bottom of the cup. Cover with a small amount of the brown sugar filling. Top with some of the remaining pecans. Repeat until all the dough, pecans and filling are used.

Bake at 350 degrees for 30 minutes. Remove from the cups to a wire rack to cool completely.

Yield: 4 to 5 dozen

A jewel of urban revitalization, New Bern has a myriad of shops, restaurants, and waterfront activities that are ablaze with gold, bronze, and other colored chrysanthemums. Even area farmers take a brief respite from their harvest duties and relax with their families while enjoying Mumfest. Tryon Palace's grounds and pampered gardens are open without charge, allowing visitors to roam the breathtaking profusion of fall blossoms.

CELEBRATING THE HARVEST

SOUP
Holiday Oyster Stew

SALADS
Autumn Tossed Salad
Carolina Peanut Vinaigrette

MAIN DISHES
Hatteras Meat Loaf
Crown Pork Roast with Cranberry Orange Stuffing
Apple Raisin Pork Chops
Yacht Club Turkey

SIDE DISHES
Granddaddy's Collards
Corn Casserole
Cranberry Apple Casserole
Southern-Style Sweet Potatoes

BREAD
Pumpkin Bread

DESSERTS
Hot Fudge Pudding Cake
Sweet Potato Pie
No-Bake Cookies

HOLIDAY OYSTER STEW

4 (12-ounce) containers fresh oysters
1/2 cup (1 stick) butter or margarine
21/2 cups sliced fresh mushrooms
1 cup chopped celery
1 cup chopped green onions
1/2 cup flour
2 cups chablis or other dry white wine
11/2 tablespoons chicken bouillon granules
1 cup heavy cream
1/4 cup grated Parmesan cheese
1/4 teaspoon thyme
1/4 teaspoon nutmeg
1/4 teaspoon pepper

Drain the oysters, reserving 2 cups of the liquid; set aside.

Melt the butter in a Dutch oven over medium heat. Add the mushrooms, celery and green onions. Cook until tender, stirring constantly. Reduce the heat to low. Add the flour. Cook for 1 minute, stirring constantly.

Stir in the reserved oyster liquid and wine gradually. Add the bouillon granules. Cook over medium heat until thickened and bubbly, stirring constantly. Stir in the oysters, cream, Parmesan cheese, thyme, nutmeg and pepper. Cook over low heat until the edges of the oysters curl and the mixture is heated through; do not boil.

Yield: 8 to 10 servings

Autumn Tossed Salad

1   head lettuce, torn, or 1 package mesclun mix
3   tart red apples or pears, unpeeled, sliced
1   small red onion, thinly sliced
1/2   cup Italian Dressing (at left)
2   ounces bleu cheese, crumbled

Toss the lettuce, apples and onion in a salad bowl. Pour the Italian Dressing over the salad and toss. Top with the bleu cheese.

Yield: 4 servings

Carolina Peanut Vinaigrette

3   tablespoons creamy peanut butter (regular or low-fat)
1/2   cup plus 2 tablespoons cider vinegar
2   tablespoons brown sugar
1 1/2 teaspoons minced garlic
1 1/4 cups peanut oil
2   teaspoons minced fresh parsley
2   teaspoons minced fresh basil
1/2   teaspoon freshly ground pepper

Whisk the peanut butter and vinegar in a bowl. Stir in the brown sugar and garlic. Add the peanut oil slowly, whisking vigorously until well mixed. Stir in the parsley, basil and pepper. Use immediately or cover and refrigerate. If the dressing begins to separate, stir before using.

Serve over mixed greens garnished with crushed unsalted dry roasted peanuts and crumbled feta or bleu cheese.

Yield: 2 cups

Hatteras Meat Loaf

1   cup each prepared mustard, barbecue sauce and port
1/2 cup cold coffee
1   tablespoon bourbon
1   pound lean ground beef
8   ounces each lean ground pork and ground veal
1 1/2 cups quick-cooking oats
1/2 cup each chili sauce and sour cream or puréed cottage cheese
2   eggs, beaten
2   tablespoons Worcestershire sauce
1   tablespoon (heaping) instant minced onions
1   teaspoon salt
1/2 teaspoon freshly ground pepper
1/4 teaspoon allspice
1/8 teaspoon each coriander and cardamom
1/2 cup chopped fresh parsley

Combine the mustard, barbecue sauce, port, coffee and bourbon in a saucepan and mix well. Bring to a boil. Reduce the heat to low. Simmer until reduced by one-third. Cool; set aside.

Combine the beef, pork and veal in a large bowl and mix well. Add the oats, chili sauce, sour cream, eggs, Worcestershire sauce, onions, salt, pepper, allspice, coriander and cardamom and mix well. Form into a 3×4×8-inch loaf. Place in a greased 9×13-inch baking dish. Cover with foil. Chill for 2 hours. Remove from the refrigerator and bring to room temperature.

Bake, covered, at 350 degrees for 1 hour. Drain off any juices, using a paper towel to absorb any moisture on the surface. Spoon half the sauce over the meat loaf.

Bake, uncovered, for 30 to 40 minutes or until the glaze is a dark reddish brown and the meat loaf is cooked through. Turn off the oven and partially open the door. Let the meat loaf stand in the oven for 10 minutes. Remove from the dish to a warm serving platter. Garnish with the parsley. Heat the remaining sauce and serve with the meat loaf.

Yield: 8 servings

Meat loaf, the much-maligned Midwest staple, is elevated here to new heights of gusto so as to appeal to discriminating Carolina tastes. Hatteras has taken the long-standing tradition of boat building to the next level, and this recipe does exactly the same thing for meat loaf.

CROWN PORK ROAST WITH CRANBERRY ORANGE STUFFING

1	tablespoon salt
1	tablespoon pepper
2	teaspoons thyme
1	(16-rib) crown pork roast, trimmed
	Cranberry Orange Stuffing (page 141)
1/4	cup (1/2 stick) butter
1/3	cup flour
2	(14-ounce) cans chicken broth
2	tablespoons Grand Marnier
2	tablespoons grated orange zest
	Salt and pepper to taste

Combine the 1 tablespoon salt, 1 tablespoon pepper and thyme in a bowl and mix well. Rub the pork roast with the seasonings. Place the roast, bone tips up, on a foil-lined rack in a roasting pan.

Roast at 350 degrees for 1 hour. Spoon 2 cups of the Cranberry Orange Stuffing into the center of the roast. Cover the rib tips with foil. Roast for 1 1/2 hours longer or until the stuffing registers 160 degrees on a meat thermometer. Place the remaining stuffing in a lightly greased 9×13-inch baking dish. Bake in the oven during the last 20 to 30 minutes of the roasting time. Remove the roast from the pan to a cutting board. Let stand for 10 minutes before carving.

Pour the pan drippings into a skillet. Add the butter. Heat until melted. Whisk in the flour until smooth. Cook until light brown. Stir in the broth, Grand Marnier and orange zest. Season with salt and pepper to taste. Cook until the sauce is thickened, stirring constantly.

Garnish the roast with kumquats and cranberries. Serve with the sauce.

Yield: 12 servings

CRANBERRY ORANGE STUFFING

2 cups dried cranberries
1 cup Grand Marnier or orange juice
2 pounds bulk pork sausage
2 cups chopped celery
1 1/3 cups chopped onions
1/2 cup (1 stick) butter
2 (14-ounce) cans chicken broth
1 teaspoon thyme
Salt and pepper to taste
2 (6-ounce) packages herb-seasoned stuffing mix
2 cups chopped pecans
2 tablespoons grated orange zest

Combine the cranberries and Grand Marnier in a small saucepan. Bring to a boil over medium heat. Remove from the heat; set aside.

Brown the sausage in a large skillet, stirring until crumbly. Remove the sausage to paper towels. Drain off all but 2 tablespoons of the drippings from the skillet.

Sauté the celery and onions in the sausage drippings until the onions are tender. Add the butter, broth, thyme, salt and pepper. Cook for 5 minutes or until the butter is melted, stirring frequently.

Add the cranberry mixture, sausage, stuffing mix, pecans and orange zest to the skillet and mix well.

APPLE RAISIN PORK CHOPS

4 pork chops
Salt and pepper to taste
2 tart apples, cored, sliced into 1/2-inch-thick rings
1/2 cup raisins
1/2 cup apple juice or cider

Brown the pork chops in a skillet for 5 minutes; drain off the drippings. Season the pork chops with salt and pepper.

Top each pork chop with an apple slice. Fill the centers of the apple slices with the raisins. Add the apple juice. Simmer, covered, over low heat until the pork chops are cooked through.

YACHT CLUB TURKEY

1   (12- to 14-pound) turkey
    Peanut oil for deep-frying
1   jar Luzianne Dry Cajun Mix

Remove the giblets from the turkey and rinse out the cavity.

To determine the exact amount of peanut oil to heat for deep-frying, measure and pour into a deep-fat fryer or large stockpot the amount of water needed to completely cover the turkey. Pour out the water and dry the pot. Add the same amount of oil to the pot. Heat to 325 to 350 degrees.

Pat the turkey dry. Coat inside and out with the Cajun mix to taste. Place the turkey carefully into the 325- to 350-degree oil, submerging it completely. Deep-fry for 3 1/2 minutes per pound (42 minutes for a 12-pound turkey; 49 minutes for a 14-pound turkey) or until cooked through.

Remove the turkey from the pot to a cutting board. Let stand for 15 minutes before carving.

Note: Use only peanut oil in this recipe.

Yield: 14 to 16 servings

GRANDDADDY'S COLLARDS

8 ounces salt pork
2 to 3 rutabagas, peeled and quartered
5 pounds fresh collard greens, cut crosswise into 1-inch strips
12 whole okra

Fill a large stockpot three-fourths full with water. Bring to a boil.

Score the top of the salt pork into 1-inch squares. Add to the boiling water with the rutabagas. Cook over medium-high heat for 1 hour.

Reduce the heat to low. Add the collard greens. Cook for about 2 hours, adding the okra during the last 30 minutes of cooking time. Remove the salt pork and drain. Serve with homemade pepper vinegar and crackling corn bread.

Yield: 12 servings

CORN CASSEROLE

1 (8-ounce) can whole kernel corn, drained
1 (8-ounce) can cream-style corn
1 cup sour cream
1 (8-ounce) package corn bread or muffin mix
1/2 cup (1 stick) margarine, melted

Mix the whole kernel corn, cream-style corn, sour cream, corn bread mix and margarine in a bowl. Spoon into a greased 9-inch square baking pan.

Bake at 350 degrees for 50 to 55 minutes.

Yield: 9 servings

CRANBERRY APPLE
CASSEROLE

3   cups chopped
    peeled apples
2   cups cranberries
1   cup sugar
2   tablespoons flour
1   cup pecan halves,
    chopped
1/2 cup packed brown
    sugar
1/2 cup flour
1/2 cup (1 stick)
    butter, melted

Combine the apples
and cranberries in a
bowl. Add the sugar
and 2 tablespoons
flour. Toss to mix.
Spoon into a greased
2-quart baking dish.
Combine the pecans,
brown sugar, 1/2 cup
flour and butter in a
bowl and mix well.
Sprinkle over the fruit.
Bake at 325 degrees for
30 to 40 minutes.

SOUTHERN-STYLE SWEET POTATOES

4   cups mashed cooked sweet potatoes or 2 (40-ounce) cans
    sweet potatoes, drained
1   cup sugar
2   eggs, beaten
1/2 cup (1 stick) butter, melted
1/2 cup milk
1   teaspoon vanilla extract
1/2 teaspoon cinnamon
1/2 cup packed brown sugar
1/2 cup chopped pecans
1/4 cup flour
2   tablespoons butter, melted

Beat the sweet potatoes, sugar, eggs, 1/2 cup butter, milk, vanilla and cinnamon in a mixing bowl until well blended. Spoon into a greased 2-quart baking dish.

Combine the brown sugar, pecans, flour and 2 tablespoons butter in a bowl and mix well. Sprinkle over the sweet potatoes.

Bake at 350 degrees for 25 minutes.

Yield: 12 servings

PUMPKIN BREAD

3 1/2 cups flour
3   cups sugar
2   teaspoons baking soda
1 1/2 teaspoons salt
1 1/2 teaspoons cinnamon
1   teaspoon allspice
2   cups canned pumpkin
4   eggs
1   cup vegetable oil
2/3 cup water
1   cup chopped pecans
1   cup flaked coconut

Combine the flour, sugar, baking soda, salt, cinnamon and allspice in a mixing bowl and mix well. Add the pumpkin, eggs, oil and water. Mix at low speed until well blended. Stir in the pecans and coconut. Pour into 2 greased and floured bundt pans.

Bake at 350 degrees for 1 hour or until a wooden pick inserted near the centers comes out clean. Cool in the pans for 10 minutes. Remove to wire racks to cool completely.

Yield: 32 servings

HOT FUDGE PUDDING CAKE

1 cup flour
3/4 cup sugar
3 tablespoons baking cocoa
2 teaspoons baking powder
1/4 teaspoon salt
1/2 cup milk
1/3 cup margarine, melted
1 1/2 teaspoons vanilla extract
1/2 cup sugar
1/2 cup packed brown sugar
1/4 cup baking cocoa
1 1/4 cups hot water

Combine the flour, 3/4 cup sugar, 3 tablespoons baking cocoa, baking powder and salt in a mixing bowl and mix well. Add the milk, margarine and vanilla. Beat until smooth. Pour into an 8-inch square baking pan.

Combine the 1/2 cup sugar, brown sugar and 1/4 cup baking cocoa in a small bowl and mix well. Sprinkle evenly over the batter in the pan. Pour the hot water over the top; do not stir.

Bake at 350 degrees for 40 minutes or until the center is set. Cool for 15 minutes before serving. Spoon into dessert dishes, ladling the sauce from the bottom of the pan over the top.

Yield: 8 to 10 servings

Sweet Potato Pie

3   medium sweet potatoes
2   egg whites
1   cup sugar
3/4   cup evaporated milk
2   egg yolks
1   teaspoon cinnamon
1/4   teaspoon nutmeg
1   unbaked (9-inch) deep-dish pie shell

Bake the sweet potatoes at 350 degrees for 1 hour and 10 minutes or until tender. Cool slightly; peel. Beat the egg whites in a mixing bowl until stiff peaks form; set aside. Mash the potatoes in a mixing bowl. Add the sugar, evaporated milk, egg yolks, cinnamon and nutmeg and mix well. Fold in the egg whites. Pour into the pie shell. Bake at 350 degrees for 35 to 40 minutes or until a knife inserted near the center comes out clean. Cool on a wire rack.

Yield: 8 servings

No-Bake Cookies

2   cups sugar
1/2   cup (1 stick) butter
1/2   cup milk
3   to 4 tablespoons baking cocoa
1   teaspoon vanilla extract
1/4   cup (rounded) peanut butter
3   cups rolled oats

Bring the sugar, butter, milk and baking cocoa to a gentle boil in a saucepan over medium heat. Cook for 3 to 4 minutes. Remove from the heat. Add the vanilla, peanut butter and oats immediately and mix well. Drop quickly by spoonfuls onto waxed paper. Cool completely.

Yield: 4 dozen

Homecoming Tailgate

Appetizers
Clam Dip
Smoked Oyster Pâté
Caponata
Do-Dads

Salad
Tortellini Salad with Vegetables

Main Dishes
Sloppy Joes
Crispy Golden Chicken
Portobello Mushroom Sandwiches with Rosemary Aïoli

Bread
Nanny's Date Nut Bread

Desserts
Delicious Pound Cake
Chocolate Oatmeal Cookies
Italian Twists
Oatmeal Raisin Cookies

CLAM DIP

1   (7-ounce) can minced clams
8   ounces cream cheese, softened
1   teaspoon minced onion
1/2 teaspoon salt
1/8 teaspoon pepper
    Dash of Tabasco sauce

Drain the clams, reserving 2 tablespoons of the juice. Combine the clams, reserved juice, cream cheese, onion, salt, pepper and Tabasco sauce in a bowl and mix well. Serve with crackers.

Yield: about 12 (2-tablespoon) servings

SMOKED OYSTER PÂTÉ

16 ounces cream cheese, softened
1   (4-ounce) can smoked oysters
1   small onion, minced
1   tablespoon fresh lemon juice
    Garlic powder to taste
    Chopped walnuts or pecans (optional)

Beat the cream cheese, oysters, onion, lemon juice and garlic powder in a mixing bowl. Shape into a ball. Wrap in plastic wrap. Chill until firm. Just before serving, roll in walnuts.

Note: You may substitute other seasonings for the garlic powder.

Yield: 20 (2-tablespoon) servings

 CAPONATA

1   medium eggplant, unpeeled, diced
1   medium onion, chopped
1   medium green bell pepper, chopped
1/2 cup chopped celery
2   garlic cloves, minced
1/4 cup olive oil
1   (8-ounce) can tomato sauce
1   (6-ounce) can tomato paste
3/4 cup pitted black olives, sliced
1/3 to 1/2 cup green olives, chopped
21/2 tablespoons sugar
21/2 tablespoons vinegar
1/2 teaspoon oregano
1/4 to 1/2 teaspoon hot red pepper sauce
     Salt and black pepper to taste

Sauté the eggplant, onion, bell pepper, celery and garlic in the olive oil in
a large skillet. Add the tomato sauce, tomato paste, black olives, green
olives, sugar and vinegar. Simmer for 30 minutes, stirring frequently. Stir
in the oregano, pepper sauce, salt and black pepper.

Chill, covered, for 24 hours. Serve with garlic pita chips.

Yield: about 32 (2-tablespoon) servings

DO-DADS

1   (12-ounce) box Cheerios cereal
1   (12-ounce) box Corn Chex cereal
1   (10-ounce) bag small pretzel twists
3   cups pecan halves
1 1/2 cups (3 sticks) margarine, melted
3   tablespoons Worcestershire sauce
3   tablespoons garlic salt

Combine the Cheerios, Corn Chex, pretzels and pecans in a bowl and mix well. Combine the margarine, Worcestershire sauce and garlic salt in a bowl and mix well. Pour over the cereal mixture and mix well. Spread out on a baking sheet.

Bake at 200 degrees for 2 1/2 hours, stirring every 15 minutes.

Yield: about 25 cups

TORTELLINI SALAD WITH VEGETABLES

1   pound frozen or refrigerated tortellini
1/2 yellow bell pepper, diced
1/2 red bell pepper, diced
1   cup frozen peas, thawed
1   small zucchini, julienned
1/2 small red onion, chopped
3/4 cup creamy Italian salad dressing

Cook the tortellini according to the package directions just until tender; drain. Rinse under cold running water; drain again.

Combine the tortellini, bell peppers, peas, zucchini, onion and salad dressing in a bowl, tossing well. Serve at room temperature or chilled.

Yield: 12 servings

CRISPY GOLDEN CHICKEN

2 eggs, beaten
1/4 cup (1/2 stick) butter, melted
1/4 teaspoon salt, minced garlic and Worcestershire sauce
1/2 teaspoon Tabasco sauce
1/8 teaspoon pepper
8 ounces barbecue potato chips, crushed
1 (3-pound) chicken, cut into 8 pieces

Combine the first 7 ingredients in a shallow bowl. Dip the chicken pieces 1 at a time in the egg mixture. Dredge in the potato chip crumbs. Place the chicken in a shallow 9×13-inch baking dish. Bake at 350 degrees for 1 hour or until tender.

SLOPPY JOES

1 pound ground beef
1 small onion, chopped
2 celery ribs, chopped
1 green bell pepper, diced
1 (10-ounce) can tomato soup
1/2 cup barbecue sauce
3/4 cup cracker crumbs
1 tablespoon Worcestershire sauce
1 teaspoon prepared mustard
1/2 teaspoon chili powder
1/8 teaspoon garlic powder
 Salt and pepper to taste
6 hamburger buns

Brown the ground beef in a skillet, stirring until crumbly; drain. Add the onion, celery and bell pepper. Cook until tender. Spoon the ground beef mixture into a slow cooker. Add the soup, barbecue sauce, cracker crumbs, Worcestershire sauce, mustard, chili powder, garlic powder, salt and pepper and mix well.

Cook on High for 2 to 3 hours. Reduce the heat to Low. Cook for 5 to 6 hours. Spoon over the hamburger buns.

Note: You may cook on top of the stove in a skillet; simmer for 30 minutes.

Yield: 6 servings

PORTOBELLO MUSHROOM SANDWICHES WITH ROSEMARY AÏOLI

1/4 cup sugar
2 tablespoons balsamic vinegar
4 (4- to 5-inch diameter) portobello mushrooms, stems removed
1 red onion, thinly sliced
3 tablespoons olive oil
  Salt and pepper to taste
4 kaiser rolls, halved
2 tablespoons olive oil
  Rosemary Aïoli (at right)
8 ounces watercress, chopped

Combine the sugar and balsamic vinegar in a small heavy saucepan. Cook over medium heat until the sugar dissolves, stirring frequently. Bring to a simmer. Simmer for 3 minutes or until slightly thickened and reduced. Cover and keep warm.

Brush the mushroom caps and onion slices on both sides with 3 tablespoons olive oil. Sprinkle with salt and pepper. Place on a grill rack over hot coals. Grill for 4 minutes on each side or until tender and cooked through. You may broil the mushroom caps and onion slices instead of grilling. Place on a platter and cover.

Brush the cut sides of the rolls with 2 tablespoons olive oil. Place on a grill rack, cut sides down, over hot coals. Grill for 2 minutes or until lightly toasted. You may broil the rolls instead of grilling.

Spread 1 tablespoon of the Rosemary Aïoli over the cut side of the rolls. Layer 1/4 cup watercress, 1 mushroom cap and one-fourth of the onion over the aïoli on the bottom side of each roll. Drizzle 1 teaspoon of the balsamic vinegar mixture over the onion, reserving the remainder for another use. Place the top half of each roll over the layers.

Yield: 4 servings

ROSEMARY AÏOLI

2 tablespoons olive oil
5 garlic cloves, unpeeled
1 tablespoon fresh lemon juice
1 tablespoon minced fresh rosemary, or 2 teaspoons dried rosemary
2 teaspoons Dijon mustard
1/2 cup mayonnaise
  Salt and pepper

Drizzle 1 tablespoon of the oil over the garlic in a baking dish. Bake, covered, at 350 degrees for 20 minutes or until tender. Cool slightly; peel. Blend the garlic, remaining olive oil, lemon juice, rosemary and mustard. Whisk with the mayonnaise in a bowl. Season with salt and pepper.

NANNY'S DATE NUT BREAD

1 cup each boiling coffee and chopped dates
1 teaspoon baking soda
1¹/2 cups flour
1 cup each sugar and chopped walnuts
1 egg
1 tablespoon butter, softened
1 teaspoon vanilla extract
   Pinch of salt

Mix the coffee, dates and baking soda in a bowl. Mix the remaining ingredients in a bowl. Add the date mixture and mix. Pour into a greased 4×8-inch loaf pan. Bake at 300 degrees for 1¹/2 hours or until bread tests done. Cool on a wire rack.

DELICIOUS POUND CAKE

1 cup (2 sticks) butter, softened
¹/2 cup shortening
3 cups sugar
5 eggs
3 cups flour
¹/2 teaspoon baking powder
¹/8 teaspoon salt
1 cup milk
1 teaspoon vanilla extract
1 teaspoon butter flavoring
1 teaspoon lemon flavoring

Cream the butter and shortening in a mixing bowl until light and fluffy. Beat in the sugar. Add the eggs 1 at a time, mixing well after each addition.

Sift the flour, baking powder and salt together. Add to the creamed mixture alternately with the milk, mixing well after each addition. Stir in the vanilla, butter flavoring and lemon flavoring. Pour into a well-greased and floured tube pan.

Bake at 300 degrees for 1 hour or until the cake tests done. Cool in the pan for 10 minutes. Invert onto a serving plate.

Yield: 16 servings

CHOCOLATE OATMEAL COOKIES

2   cups sugar
1/2 cup (1 stick) margarine
1/2 cup milk
1/4 cup baking cocoa
1/4 teaspoon salt
31/2 cups quick-cooking oats
1/2 cup peanut butter
1   teaspoon vanilla extract

Combine the sugar, margarine, milk, baking cocoa and salt in a large saucepan. Cook over medium heat until the sugar is dissolved, stirring constantly. Bring to a rolling boil. Remove from the heat. Stir in the oats, peanut butter and vanilla and mix well. Drop by teaspoonfuls onto waxed paper. Cool completely. Store in an airtight container.

Yield: 4 dozen

ITALIAN TWISTS

4   cups flour
4   eggs
1/2 cup (1 stick) butter, softened
1   teaspoon each salt and vanilla extract
     Vegetable oil for deep-frying
1   cup confectioners' sugar

Mix the flour, eggs, butter, salt and vanilla in a bowl to form a dough. Knead until well mixed. Roll out 1/4 inch thick on a lightly floured surface. Cut into 1×4-inch pieces. Tie each piece into a bow.

Deep-fry in 365-degree oil until golden brown on both sides. Drain on paper towels. Dust with confectioners' sugar.

Yield: about 4 dozen

OATMEAL RAISIN COOKIES

3/4   cup (1 1/2 sticks) unsalted butter, softened
1 1/2 cups maple sugar
2   eggs
1   teaspoon vanilla extract
1 1/2 cups unbleached flour
1   teaspoon baking soda
1   teaspoon cinnamon
1/2   teaspoon salt
1   cup rolled oats
1   cup organic raisins

Cream the butter and maple sugar in a mixing bowl until light and fluffy. Beat in the eggs and vanilla.

Sift the flour, baking soda, cinnamon and salt into a medium bowl. Add the oats and toss to mix. Stir into the creamed mixture with a wooden spoon just until blended. Mix in the raisins.

Shape by heaping tablespoonfuls into mounds. Place 2 inches apart on 2 parchment-lined cookie sheets.

Bake 1 sheet at a time at 325 degrees for 13 minutes or until the centers have risen and the bottoms are golden brown. Cool on the cookie sheet for 1 minute. Remove to a wire rack to cool completely.

Yield: about 3 dozen

WINTER

ON A
*W*INTER'S
NIGHT

During the Colonial period, families would bask in the fire's glow with a glass of hot mulled cider or chocolate to ward off the winter's chill. Governor Tryon, the Colonial Governor of the North Carolina colony, would have served his guests two main courses with a variety of roasted meats accompanied by relishes made from the summer garden's bounty. The dinner finished with two dessert courses. Or, perhaps during the Christmas season, an elegant supper would be served to celebrate the Twelfth Night when three kings arrived in Bethlehem bearing their gifts for the Christ Child. The Twelfth Night Cake, still made today, announces "The King for the Evening" with a royal flair.

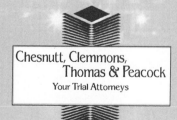

Chesnutt, Clemmons,
Thomas & Peacock
Your Trial Attorneys

SUPER BOWL

PAGE 161

BEST FRIENDS, BIRTHDAY BASHES
AND THE COTILLION

PAGE 170

COASTAL CAROLINA CHRISTMAS

PAGE 182

BEST FRIENDS, BIRTHDAY BASHES
AND THE COTILLION

Super Bowl

Appetizers

Sausage and Cheese Puffs

Spicy Chili Cheese Dip

Hot Cheddar Bean Dip

Salad

Sesame Chicken with Bow Tie Pasta

Soups

Pantry Soup

Chili

Main Dishes

Hot Chopped Spinach Casserole

BBQ Spareribs with Homemade Barbecue Sauce

Chicken Enchiladas

Bread

Boston Brown Bread

Desserts

Praline Pecan Crunch

Chocolate Chip Cake

Orange Balls

SAUSAGE AND CHEESE PUFFS

1   pound bulk pork sausage
1   cup shredded Cheddar cheese
1 1/2 cups baking mix
1   cup water

Brown the sausage in a skillet, stirring until crumbly; drain and cool.

Combine the sausage and cheese in a bowl. Stir in the baking mix and water gradually. Shape into balls. Place on a greased baking sheet.

Bake at 350 degrees for 10 to 15 minutes or until browned.

Yield: about 3 dozen

SPICY CHILI CHEESE DIP

2   (16-ounce) jars Cheez Whiz
2   (16-ounce) jars salsa or picante sauce
1   pound mild bulk pork sausage

Remove the lids from the jars of Cheez Whiz. Microwave the Cheez Whiz until warm. Place in a slow cooker. Stir in the salsa.

Brown the sausage in a skillet, stirring until crumbly; drain. Add to the salsa mixture and mix well.

Cook on High for 15 to 20 minutes or until hot. Serve with tortilla chips.

Note: You may add shredded cheese, sour cream, and/or hot red pepper sauce to taste.

Yield: 80 (2-tablespoon) servings

HOT CHEDDAR BEAN DIP

1   (16-ounce) can pinto beans, drained, mashed
1   cup shredded Cheddar cheese
1/2 cup mayonnaise
1   (4-ounce) can chopped green chiles
1/4 teaspoon hot red pepper sauce

Combine the beans, cheese, mayonnaise, chiles and pepper sauce in a bowl, mixing well. Spoon into a 3-cup baking dish.

Bake at 350 degrees for 30 minutes or until bubbly.

Yield: 20 (2-tablespoon) servings

SESAME CHICKEN WITH BOW TIE PASTA

1/2 cup vegetable oil
2   tablespoons sesame seeds
6   ounces bow tie pasta, cooked, drained
3   cups chopped cooked chicken
1/2 cup chopped green onions
1/2 cup chopped fresh parsley
1/3 cup white wine vinegar
2   tablespoons sugar
1/4 teaspoon pepper

Heat the oil in a skillet. Add the sesame seeds. Cook until toasted, stirring constantly.

Combine the sesame seeds, pasta, chicken, green onions, parsley, vinegar, sugar and pepper in a bowl and mix well. Chill until cold.

Yield: 4 servings

PANTRY SOUP

1   pound ground beef
2   cups uncooked macaroni or other pasta
4   cups water
1   (28-ounce) can crushed tomatoes
1   (16-ounce) can pinto beans
1   (15-ounce) can whole kernel corn, drained
1   envelope taco seasoning mix
1   to 2 tablespoons Tabasco sauce
    Shredded Cheddar cheese (optional)

Brown the ground beef in a Dutch oven over medium-high heat, stirring until crumbly; drain. Add the next 7 ingredients. Bring to a boil. Reduce the heat to low. Simmer, covered, for 30 minutes. Ladle into bowls and garnish with cheese.

Yield: 4 to 6 servings

CHILI

2   pounds ground beef
1   medium onion, finely chopped
3   (15-ounce) cans kidney beans
2   (15-ounce) cans stewed tomatoes
1   cup medium salsa
3   tablespoons chili powder
2   tablespoons brown sugar
1   teaspoon each basil and oregano
1/2 teaspoon celery seeds
    Seasoned salt and pepper to taste

Brown the ground beef with the onion in a skillet, stirring until the ground beef is crumbly; drain. Combine the ground beef mixture and the remaining ingredients in a stockpot and mix well. Bring to a boil. Reduce the heat to low. Simmer for 1 hour or longer.

Yield: 12 servings

Hot Chopped Spinach Casserole

1	pound ground beef
1	pound spicy bulk pork sausage
1	small onion, chopped
1	(10-ounce) package frozen chopped spinach, thawed, drained
1	(10-ounce) can cream of chicken soup
1	cup sour cream
8	ounces sliced fresh mushrooms
1/2	cup instant rice
1/8 to 1/4	teaspoon oregano
1/2	teaspoon minced garlic
8	ounces Monterey Jack cheese, shredded
8	ounces Cheddar cheese, shredded

Brown the ground beef and sausage with the onion in a large skillet, stirring until the ground beef and sausage are crumbly; drain.

Add the spinach, soup, sour cream, mushrooms, rice, oregano and garlic and mix well. Spoon into a lightly greased 2-quart baking dish. Sprinkle the Monterey Jack cheese and Cheddar cheese over the top.

Bake at 350 degrees for 45 minutes to 1 hour.

Yield: 6 to 8 servings

HOMEMADE BARBECUE SAUCE

1¹/2 cups ketchup
1¹/2 cups water
1   cup packed brown sugar
1   cup vinegar
1   tablespoon Worcestershire sauce
1   tablespoon crushed red pepper

Combine the ketchup, water, brown sugar, vinegar, Worcestershire sauce and crushed red pepper in a medium saucepan. Bring to a boil. Reduce the heat to low. Simmer for 15 minutes.

Note: May add more or less ketchup to achieve the desired consistency.

BBQ SPARERIBS WITH HOMEMADE BARBECUE SAUCE

6   pounds spareribs
¹/4 cup prepared mustard
¹/4 cup chili sauce
¹/4 cup vegetable oil
¹/4 cup packed brown sugar
¹/4 cup Worcestershire sauce
     Homemade Barbecue Sauce (at left)

Place the ribs in a greased 9×13-inch baking pan. Combine the mustard, chili sauce, oil, brown sugar and Worcestershire sauce in a medium bowl and mix well. Pour over the ribs. Cover the pan with foil.

Bake at 350 degrees for 45 minutes or until cooked through. Serve with Homemade Barbecue Sauce.

Yield: 8 servings

CHICKEN ENCHILADAS

1   (10-ounce) can fat-free cream of chicken soup
1/2   cup fat-free sour cream
2   tablespoons margarine
1/2   cup chopped onion
1   teaspoon chili powder
2   cups diced cooked chicken
1   (4-ounce) can chopped green chiles
8   flour tortillas
1   cup shredded Cheddar cheese

Combine the soup and sour cream in a small bowl and mix until smooth; set aside.

Melt the margarine in a 2-quart saucepan over medium heat. Add the onion and chili powder. Cook until the onion is tender. Stir in the chicken, chiles and 2 tablespoons of the soup mixture. Remove from the heat.

Spoon about 1/4 cup of the chicken filling down the center of each tortilla. Fold in the sides of the tortillas over the filling. Place seam side down in a greased 8×12-inch baking dish. Spread the remaining soup mixture over the enchiladas. Cover with foil.

Bake at 375 degrees for 15 minutes. Uncover. Sprinkle with the cheese. Bake, uncovered, for 5 minutes longer or until the cheese melts. Garnish with chopped fresh parsley. Serve with a tossed salad.

Yield: 10 servings

Boston Brown bread

1   cup flour
1   teaspoon each baking powder, baking soda and salt
1   cup each cornmeal and whole wheat flour
2   cups buttermilk
3/4 cup molasses
1/2 cup shortening
2   eggs
1   cup raisins

Mix the first 4 ingredients in a bowl. Stir in the cornmeal and whole wheat flour. Add the buttermilk, molasses, shortening, eggs and raisins and beat well. Spoon into 4 greased and floured 1-pound food cans. Cover each can with a piece of greased foil. Place the cans on a rack in a deep ovenproof pot. Pour in enough water to come about 1/2 inch up the sides of the cans. Bake, covered, at 325 degrees for 3 hours. Remove the cans from the pot. Let stand for 10 minutes. Remove the bread from the cans.

Yield: 24 servings

Praline pecan crunch

1   (16-ounce) box Quaker Oat Squares cereal (8 cups)
2   cups pecan pieces
1/2 cup each light corn syrup and packed brown sugar
1/4 cup (1/2 stick) margarine
1   teaspoon vanilla extract
1/2 teaspoon baking soda

Mix the cereal and pecans in a 9×13-inch baking pan. Place the next 3 ingredients in a 2-cup microwave-safe bowl. Microwave on High for 1 1/2 minutes; stir. Microwave on High for 30 seconds to 1 1/2 minutes or until boiling. Stir in the vanilla and baking soda. Pour over the cereal mixture. Stir to coat evenly. Bake at 250 degrees for 1 hour, stirring every 20 minutes. Spread on a baking sheet to cool. Break into pieces.

Yield: 10 cups

CHOCOLATE CHIP CAKE

Cake

1   (2-layer) package butter chocolate cake mix
1/2   cup (1 stick) butter, softened
4   eggs
1 1/4 cups water
1   (3-ounce) package chocolate instant pudding mix
1   cup chocolate chips

Cream Cheese Icing

3   ounces cream cheese, softened
1   tablespoon milk
2 1/2 cups confectioners' sugar
1   teaspoon vanilla extract
    Dash of salt

For the cake, beat the cake mix, butter, eggs, water and pudding mix in a mixing bowl until well blended. Stir in the chocolate chips. Pour into a greased bundt pan.

Bake at 325 degrees for 45 minutes. Reduce the oven temperature to 300 degrees. Bake for 10 minutes or until the cake tests done. Cool in the pan for 10 minutes. Invert onto a serving plate. Cool completely.

For the icing, beat the cream cheese and milk in a mixing bowl. Add the confectioners' sugar gradually, beating well. Stir in the vanilla and salt. Spread the icing over the top and side of the cooled cake.

Yield: 16 servings

ORANGE BALLS

1   (12-ounce) package vanilla wafers, finely crushed
1   (1-pound) package confectioners' sugar
1   cup chopped pecans
1/2   cup (1 stick) margarine, softened
1   (6-ounce) can orange juice concentrate, thawed
1   (14-ounce) bag flaked coconut

Combine the vanilla wafer crumbs, confectioners' sugar, pecans, margarine and juice concentrate in a bowl. Form into balls. Roll in coconut to coat. Place on waxed paper until firm.

Best Friends, Birthday Bashes and the Cotillion

Appetizer
Carolina Crab Cakes

Soup
Chicken Vegetable Soup

Salad
Kiwi, Strawberry and Chicken Salad

Main Dishes
Celebration Glazed Ham
Roast Pork with Brie and Apples
Hamburger Casserole
Chicken with Feather-Light Dumplings
Chicken Casserole

Side Dishes
Mashed Potatoes
Pickett Duffy's Spinach Soufflé
Baked Macaroni and Cheese

Desserts
Super Seven-Up Cake • Chocolate Éclair
Fruit Dip
Peanut Brittle • Spanish Cream

CAROLINA CRAB CAKES

2 pounds jumbo lump crab meat
2 eggs
1/2 cup minced green onions
1 tablespoon mayonnaise
1 teaspoon mustard
1 1/2 teaspoons Old Bay seasoning
1 teaspoon baking powder
3 tablespoons dried seasoned bread crumbs
  Flour
1 cup olive or peanut oil
  Remoulade Sauce (page 172)

Remove and discard the shells from the crab meat. Place the crab meat in a bowl, being careful not to shred the crab meat. Chill.

Whisk the eggs, green onions, mayonnaise and mustard in a bowl. Fold in the Old Bay seasoning, baking powder and bread crumbs. Chill.

Fold the crab meat gently into the mayonnaise mixture. Chill for about 10 minutes.

Form the crab mixture into 3-ounce cakes. (May be prepared 1 day ahead of time, covered and refrigerated.)

Dust the crab cakes in flour to coat. Heat the olive oil in a nonstick skillet over medium heat for 3 to 4 minutes. Add the crab cakes. Fry for 2 minutes on each side or until golden brown. Remove from the skillet; drain on paper towels. Just before serving, rewarm in a 300-degree oven for 5 minutes.

To serve, place 2 crab cakes on each plate. Serve with Remoulade Sauce and lemon wedges.

Yield: 12 servings

RÉMOULADE SAUCE

1/4   teaspoon basil
1/4   teaspoon thyme
1/4   teaspoon garlic powder
1/4   teaspoon onion powder
1/4   teaspoon crushed red pepper
1/4   teaspoon chili powder
1/4   teaspoon salt
1/4   teaspoon black pepper
1   bay leaf
1 1/2 cups mayonnaise
1   teaspoon minced celery
1   teaspoon minced scallions
1   teaspoon capers
1   teaspoon horseradish
1   teaspoon whole-grain mustard
1   teaspoon Worcestershire sauce
4   drops of Tabasco sauce
      Juice of 1/2 lemon

Place the basil, thyme, garlic powder, onion powder, crushed red pepper, chili powder, salt, black pepper and bay leaf in a coffee grinder. Process until finely ground.

Combine the mayonnaise, celery, scallions, capers, horseradish, mustard, Worcestershire sauce, Tabasco sauce and spice mixture in a medium bowl and mix well. Fold in the lemon juice.

Yield: 12 servings

CHICKEN VEGETABLE SOUP

3   tablespoons olive oil
3   cups sliced carrots
2   cups sliced celery
1   onion, chopped
1   tablespoon plus 1 1/2 teaspoons minced garlic
2   tablespoons basil
1   tablespoon fresh cracked pepper
4   boneless skinless chicken breast halves, cut into bite-size pieces
1   (14-ounce) can diced Italian-style tomatoes
12 cups chicken broth
6   cups water
1   (10-ounce) package frozen chopped spinach, thawed
1   tablespoon balsamic vinegar
8   ounces uncooked small bow tie pasta

Heat the olive oil in a large stockpot over medium-high heat. Add the carrots, celery, onion, garlic, basil, pepper and chicken. Cook for 10 to 15 minutes or until the vegetables are almost tender and the chicken is almost cooked.

Add the tomatoes, broth, water, spinach and vinegar. Bring to a boil. Reduce the heat to low. Simmer for 15 minutes. Return the soup to a boil. Stir in the pasta. Cook just until the pasta is tender yet firm.

Serve with grated Parmesan cheese and crusty Italian bread.

Note: You may substitute fresh kale for the spinach. May also add 2 cans of dark red kidney beans or cannellini.

Yield: 12 servings

KIWI, STRAWBERRY AND CHICKEN SALAD

2   pints fresh strawberries, sliced
3   cups chopped cooked chicken
3   kiwifruit, sliced
1   cup sliced toasted almonds
    Poppy Seed Dressing (at left)
6   cups torn fresh spinach leaves

Combine the strawberries, chicken, kiwifruit, almonds and Poppy Seed Dressing in a bowl and toss to coat with dressing. Arrange the spinach leaves on salad plates. Top with the chicken mixture.

Yield: 8 servings

CELEBRATION GLAZED HAM

1   (8- to 10-pound) ham (shank half or butt portion)
2   (8-ounce) cans crushed pineapple
1   (1-pound) package light brown sugar
1   to 2 (20-ounce) cans sliced pineapple, drain, reserving 1/2 juice
    Whole cloves (optional)
1   (16-ounce) jar maraschino cherries, drain, reserving juice

Pour enough water into a roasting pan to reach a 1-inch depth. Place the ham in the pan. Cover with foil. Bake at 350 degrees for 11/2 to 2 hours or to 125 degrees on a meat thermometer. Combine the crushed pineapple and brown sugar in a bowl. Remove the ham from the oven. Score the surface. Spread some of the pineapple mixture into the crevices on the ham. Spread the remaining mixture over the top. Arrange the pineapple slices over the ham, securing them with wooden picks. Place a clove inside the center of each pineapple slice. Place a cherry inside the center of each pineapple slice, securing with wooden picks. Insert desired amount of cloves. Drizzle the reserved pineapple and cherry juice over the ham. Bake, uncovered, for 30 minutes.

Yield: 16 to 20 servings

174

ROAST PORK WITH BRIE AND APPLES

4 ounces bacon, coarsely chopped
1 red apple, diced
1 medium yellow onion, diced
3 pounds center-cut pork tenderloin
6 ounces Brie cheese, diagonally sliced

Cook the bacon, apple and onion in a skillet over medium heat until the bacon is crisp. Remove to a bowl. Refrigerate until cool. Cut a pocket in the pork tenderloin. Combine the bacon mixture and the cheese and mix well. Stuff into the pocket. Tie the pocket closed with 4 pieces of butcher's string. Place in a roasting pan. Roast at 350 degrees for 35 minutes or to 160 degrees on a meat thermometer. Let stand for 10 minutes before carving.

Yield: 8 servings

HAMBURGER CASSEROLE

2 pounds ground beef
1 cup chopped onion
1/2 cup chopped celery
12 ounces noodles, cooked, drained
2 (10-ounce) cans tomato soup
1 teaspoon Worcestershire sauce
10 ounces Cheddar cheese, shredded

Brown the ground beef with the onion and celery in a skillet, stirring until the ground beef is crumbly; drain. Layer the beef mixture and noodles alternately in a greased 4-quart baking dish, ending with the noodles. Combine the tomato soup and Worcestershire sauce in a bowl. Pour over the noodles. Top with the cheese. Bake at 350 degrees for 45 minutes.

Yield: 14 servings

FEATHER-LIGHT DUMPLINGS

1 cup flour
1/2 cup bread crumbs
2 teaspoons baking
   powder
1/4 teaspoon salt
   Pepper to taste
1/3 cup milk
1/4 cup chopped onion
1 egg, well beaten
2 tablespoons butter,
   melted
1 tablespoon chopped
   fresh parsley

Mix the flour, bread crumbs, baking powder, salt and pepper in a bowl. Mix the milk, onion, egg, butter and parsley in a separate bowl. Add to the dry ingredients and mix well.

CHICKEN WITH FEATHER-LIGHT DUMPLINGS

1 (3-pound) chicken, cut up
1 tablespoon vegetable oil
2 carrots, thinly sliced
1 rib celery, chopped
1 onion, chopped
1 (10-ounce) can cream of mushroom soup
1 1/4 cups water
1/2 teaspoon thyme
   Salt and pepper to taste
   Feather-Light Dumplings (at left)

Brown the chicken in the oil in a Dutch oven. Remove and set aside.

Add the carrots, celery and onion to the Dutch oven. Sauté until tender. Stir in the soup, water, thyme, salt and pepper. Return the chicken to the Dutch oven. Bring to a boil. Reduce the heat to low. Simmer, covered, for 30 minutes or until the chicken is cooked through.

Drop the Feather-Light Dumplings dough by spoonfuls on top of the chicken mixture. Simmer, covered, for 20 minutes longer.

Note: You may substitute 1 cup baking mix prepared according to the package directions for dumplings for the Feather-Light Dumplings.

Yield: 4 servings

Chicken Casserole

1   (3-pound) chicken, cooked, boned
1/2   cup (1 stick) butter, melted
1   (14-ounce) package stuffing mix
1   cup sour cream
1   (10-ounce) can cream of mushroom soup
1   cup chicken broth

Chop the cooled chicken; set aside. Mix the butter and stuffing mix in a bowl. Mix the sour cream and soup in a separate bowl. Spoon 1/2 of the stuffing mixture into a 3-quart baking dish. Layer the chicken, sour cream mixture and remaining stuffing mixture in the dish. Pour the broth over the top.

Bake at 350 degrees for 45 minutes.

Yield: 10 servings

Mashed Potatoes

1   (5-pound) bag potatoes, peeled, coarsely chopped
8   ounces cream cheese, softened
1   cup sour cream
2   tablespoons butter, softened
    Salt and pepper to taste
    Milk

Combine the potatoes with enough water to cover in a saucepan. Bring to a boil. Boil until tender; drain. Return the potatoes to the saucepan.

Add the cream cheese, sour cream, butter, salt, pepper and a small amount of milk. Mash until smooth, adding more milk as needed.

Note: You may store the mashed potatoes in the refrigerator for up to 10 days or in the freezer.

Yield: 20 servings

PICKETT DUFFY'S SPINACH SOUFFLÉ

3   (10-ounce) packages frozen chopped spinach
2   cups sour cream
1   envelope onion soup mix

Cook the spinach according to the package directions; drain well.

Combine the spinach, sour cream and soup mix in a bowl. Spoon into a greased 1¹/2-quart baking dish.

Bake at 350 degrees for 30 minutes.

Note: You may refrigerate or freeze after assembling. Bring to room temperature before baking.

Yield: 10 servings

BAKED MACARONI AND CHEESE

2   cups shredded Cheddar cheese
¹/4   cup (¹/2 stick) margarine
7   ounces elbow macaroni, cooked, drained
2   eggs, beaten
1   cup (or more) milk

Place the cheese in the bottom of a 2-quart baking dish. Top with pats of margarine. Add the cooked macaroni on top and mix well. Stir in the eggs. Add enough milk so that the mixture has a soupy consistency.

Bake at 400 degrees until heated through and lightly browned.

Note: Do not overcook the macaroni.

Yield: 12 servings

Super Seven-Up Cake

1 1/2 cups (3 sticks) butter, softened
3   cups sugar
5   eggs
3   cups flour
2   tablespoons lemon extract
1   cup Seven-Up

Cream the butter and sugar in a mixing bowl at medium speed until light and fluffy. Add the eggs 1 at a time, beating well after each addition. Add the flour and mix well. Beat in the lemon extract and Seven-Up. Pour into a well-greased and floured bundt pan.

Bake at 325 degrees for 1 1/4 hours or until the cake tests done. Cool in the pan for 10 minutes. Invert onto a serving plate to cool completely. Frost with your favorite icing and decorate as desired.

Yield: 16 servings

Chocolate Éclair

1   (16-ounce) package graham crackers
2   (3-ounce) packages French vanilla instant pudding mix
3   cups milk
12 ounces whipped topping
1   (16-ounce) can chocolate frosting, melted

Line the bottom of a 9×13-inch baking pan with graham crackers.

Combine the pudding mix and milk in a mixing bowl. Beat for about 2 minutes. Stir in the whipped topping. Layer 1/2 the pudding mixture, graham crackers, remaining pudding mixture and graham crackers in the pan. Top with the melted chocolate frosting. Refrigerate, covered, for 8 to 12 hours.

Yield: 10 servings

FRUIT DIP

8   ounces cream cheese, softened
1   (7-ounce) jar marshmallow creme
1   tablespoon lemon juice
    Assorted fresh fruit, cut up

Combine the cream cheese, marshmallow creme and lemon juice in a bowl and blend well. Serve as a dip for fresh fruit.

Yield: 8 (2-tablespoon) servings

PEANUT BRITTLE

2   cups sugar
1   cup light corn syrup
1/2   cup hot water
1/2   teaspoon salt
1 1/2 cups raw peanuts
2   tablespoons butter
2   teaspoons vanilla extract
1/2   teaspoon baking soda

Combine the sugar, corn syrup, water and salt in a heavy saucepan and mix well. Bring to a boil. Add the peanuts.

Cook over medium-low heat until the mixture begins to change color. Add the butter and vanilla. Cook to 280 degrees on a candy thermometer, soft-crack stage, stirring occasionally. Remove from the heat. Stir in the baking soda. Pour onto a buttered baking sheet. Cool until set. Break into pieces.

Note: If using roasted peanuts, don't add them until the mixture reaches 280 degrees. Return the mixture to a full boil before removing from the heat.

Yield: 36 (1-ounce) servings

SPANISH CREAM

1/4 cup sugar
1 envelope unflavored gelatin
  Dash of salt
1 cup milk
2 egg yolks, slightly beaten
1 teaspoon vanilla extract
1 cup milk
2 egg whites
1/4 cup sugar

Combine 1/4 cup sugar, gelatin and salt in a small saucepan. Stir in 1 cup milk and egg yolks until well blended. Cook over low heat for 8 to 10 minutes or until the gelatin dissolves and the mixture coats a metal spoon, stirring constantly. Remove from the heat.

Stir in the vanilla and 1 cup milk. Pour into a medium bowl. Refrigerate until the consistency of unbeaten egg whites. (To hasten thickening, place in a larger bowl filled with ice water.)

Beat the egg whites in a small mixing bowl until frothy. Add 1/4 cup sugar gradually, beating until soft peaks form. Fold into the thickened gelatin mixture. Pour into a 1-quart mold or six 5-ounce custard cups. Refrigerate for 2 hours or until firm.

Loosen the edge of the mold with a spatula. Invert onto a serving dish, shaking gently to release. Garnish with sweetened whipped cream and chocolate curls or fresh strawberries.

Note: For a two-layer Spanish Cream, follow the recipe as directed, but do not refrigerate the gelatin mixture. Cool until slightly warm, then fold into the beaten egg white mixture. Pour into the mold and refrigerate until firm. The mixture will separate into 2 layers.

Yield: 6 servings

Coastal Carolina Christmas

Beverage
Cap'n Polly's Eggnog

Appetizers
Christmas Cheese Ball

Hot Cheese Puffs • Hot Crab Dip

Soups
Seafarer's Delight • Bretagne Bouillabaisse

Salads
Mixed Green Salad with Roquefort Vinaigrette

Cranberry Salad

Main Dishes
Marinated Roast Beef

Three Shepherds' Pie

Thai-Spiced Pork Tenderloin with Orange Curry Sauce

Classic Brunswick Stew • Fish Bake Casserole

Side Dishes
Cauliflower au Gratin • Cori's Sweet Potatoes

Bread
Sally Lunn Bread

Desserts
Rich Twelfth Night Cake • Angel Bars • Eula's Cake

Holiday Chocolate Nut Squares

Brown Sugar Fudge • English Trifle

CAP'N POLLY'S EGGNOG

16 egg yolks
3¹/2 cups sugar
3   quarts milk
2   pints whiskey
1   pint rum
1   pint applejack
16 egg whites
1   quart whipping cream, whipped
    Nutmeg

Combine the egg yolks, sugar and milk in a heavy saucepan. Cook over very low heat until the mixture coats a metal spoon with a thin film and reaches 160 degrees, stirring constantly. Remove from the heat. Cool slightly. Stir in the whiskey, rum and applejack.

Beat the egg whites in a mixing bowl until stiff peaks form. Fold the egg whites and whipped cream into the yolk mixture.

Store for up to 4 days in the refrigerator. Sprinkle nutmeg over each serving.

Yield: 2 gallons

CHRISTMAS CHEESE BALL

16 ounces cream cheese, softened
13 ounces shredded Cheddar cheese (sharp or medium)
2   teaspoons lemon juice
    Dash of Texas Pete hot sauce
    Dash of salt
1/2 cup finely chopped walnuts

Combine the cream cheese, Cheddar cheese, lemon juice, hot sauce and salt in a bowl and mix well. Refrigerate for 3 to 12 hours or until firm.

Shape into a ball. Roll in the walnuts. Refrigerate, covered with foil, until ready to serve.

Yield: 40 (2-tablespoon) servings

HOT CHEESE PUFFS

1   cup mayonnaise
3/4 cup grated Parmesan cheese
1   tablespoon grated onion
1   (40-slice) package party rye bread slices

Combine the mayonnaise, cheese and onion in a bowl and mix well. Spread over one side of each slice of bread. Place bread slices, spread side up, on a baking sheet. Broil until bubbly.

Yield: 40 puffs

The Coastal Carolina Christmas season begins in New Bern during the first week in December. In most of the surrounding towns, Santa Claus arrives each Christmas by fire truck. But in New Bern he arrives on a Hatteras yacht adorned with sparkling lights and seasonal decorations. To the delight of spectators, the Coastal Christmas Flotilla celebration takes place on the Trent River.

HOT CRAB DIP

16   ounces cream cheese, softened
6   tablespoons mayonnaise
1/4   cup dry white wine or vermouth
1   tablespoon Dijon mustard
1/2   teaspoon sugar
  Pinch of salt
1   pound crab meat, flaked

Combine the cream cheese, mayonnaise, wine, mustard, sugar and salt in the top of a double boiler. Place over simmering water. Cook until well blended and heated through, stirring constantly. Stir in the crab meat. Remove to a chafing dish and keep warm over low heat.

Yield: 32 (2-tablespoon) servings

SEAFARER'S DELIGHT

1   pound scallops
1   large onion, cut into thin wedges
2   tablespoons butter
1/4   cup flour
3 1/2 cups milk
1   (4-ounce) can sliced mushrooms
1   teaspoon salt
  Dash of pepper
1/2   cup each dry white wine and shredded Swiss cheese
1   tablespoon minced fresh parsley

Cut any large scallops into halves; set aside. Cook the onion in the butter in a saucepan over low heat until tender. Stir in the flour. Add the milk gradually, stirring constantly. Cook over medium heat until bubbly. Stir in the mushrooms, scallops, salt and pepper. Simmer, covered, for 5 minutes. Stir in the wine and heat through. Ladle into bowls and garnish with the cheese and parsley.

Yield: 6 servings

BRETAGNE BOUILLABAISSE

FISH STOCK

6   cups water
1   (1¹/2-pound) fresh
    or frozen dressed
    fish (with head
    and tail)

Combine the water
and fish in a large
saucepan. Bring to a
boil. Reduce the heat
to low. Simmer for 30
minutes. Strain the
stock, reserving the
cooked fish for
another use.

1   pound small lobster tails
1   pound red snapper or sole fillets
1   pound cod or haddock fillets
12   ounces scallops
1   dozen clams in shells
¹/3 cup olive or vegetable oil
2   large onions, chopped (2 cups)
6   cups Fish Stock (at left) or water
1   (28-ounce) can tomatoes, cut up
2   small garlic cloves, minced
1   tablespoon salt
2   sprigs of parsley
2   bay leaves
1¹/2 teaspoons thyme, crushed
¹/2 teaspoon saffron threads, crushed
¹/8 teaspoon pepper
     French bread slices

Split each lobster tail lengthwise into halves. Cut each piece crosswise
into halves to make 6 to 8 portions. Cut the snapper and cod fillets into
2-inch pieces. Cut any large scallops into halves. Scrub the clams well.

Heat the olive oil in a large saucepan or Dutch oven. Add the onions.
Cook until tender but not browned. Add the Fish Stock, tomatoes, garlic,
salt, parsley, bay leaves, thyme, saffron and pepper. Bring to a boil. Reduce
the heat to low. Simmer, covered, for 30 minutes. Strain the seasoned
stock into a large stockpot, discarding the vegetables and herbs.

Bring the strained stock to a boil. Add the lobster and fillet pieces. Cook
for 5 minutes. Add the scallops and clams. Boil for 5 minutes or until the
clams open. (Discard any clams that do not open.) Serve in shallow bowls
with French bread.

Note: You may use fresh or frozen fish and shellfish. If frozen, thaw first.
Cut the lobster tails when they are partially thawed.

Yield: 6 to 8 servings

MIXED GREEN SALAD WITH ROQUEFORT VINAIGRETTE

8   cups mixed baby greens
8   ounces plum tomatoes, seeded, diced
4   green onions, chopped
1/4 cup dried cranberries or currants
1/2 cup chopped pecans, toasted
1/2 cup plus 1 tablespoon olive oil
3   tablespoons raspberry or red wine vinegar
    Salt and pepper to taste
1/2 cup crumbled Roquefort cheese (about 2 ounces)

Combine the greens, tomatoes, green onions, cranberries and pecans in a large bowl.

Whisk the olive oil and vinegar in a small bowl until blended. Season with salt and pepper. Mix in the cheese. Pour the dressing over the salad. Toss to mix.

Yield: 6 servings

CRANBERRY SALAD

1   (12-ounce) bag fresh cranberries
1   cup crushed pineapple, drained
1   cup sugar
1   (16-ounce) package miniature marshmallows
12 ounces whipped topping

Process the cranberries in a food processor until ground. Remove to a bowl. Stir in the pineapple and sugar. Refrigerate, covered, for 8 to 12 hours.

Stir in the marshmallows and whipped topping when ready to serve.

Yield: 12 servings

MARINATED ROAST BEEF

1   (6- to 8-pound) beef rump roast or venison roast
1   cup olive or vegetable oil
3/4 cup Dale's steak seasoning
1/2 cup lemon juice
1/4 cup each Worcestershire sauce and prepared mustard
1/4 cup minced garlic
1   tablespoon freshly ground pepper

Pierce the roast at 1-inch intervals with a meat fork. Place in a large heavy-duty sealable plastic bag. Combine the olive oil, steak seasoning, lemon juice, Worcestershire sauce, mustard and garlic in a bowl. Pour over the roast; seal the bag. Marinate in the refrigerator for 1 to 2 days, turning the roast occasionally.

Remove the roast from the bag. Place in a roasting pan. Pour the marinade in the pan. Sprinkle the roast with the pepper. Roast at 350 degrees for 1 hour and 50 minutes or to 160 degrees on a meat thermometer. Let stand for 15 minutes before carving.

Yield: 20 to 28 servings

THREE SHEPHERDS' PIE

1   pound ground beef
1   medium onion, chopped
1   (8-ounce) can tomato sauce
1   (14-ounce) can green beans, drained
     Mashed cooked potatoes
     Shredded sharp Cheddar cheese

Brown the ground beef with the onion in a skillet, stirring until the ground beef is crumbly; drain. Stir in the tomato sauce and beans. Spoon into a 1-quart baking dish. Spread enough mashed potatoes over the top to cover. Sprinkle with the cheese. Bake at 350 degrees for 30 minutes.

Yield: 4 servings

THAI-SPICED PORK TENDERLOIN WITH ORANGE CURRY SAUCE

1/2 cup molasses
1/2 cup reduced-sodium soy sauce
1/4 cup Thai red curry base
1 tablespoon grated gingerroot
1 1/2 pounds pork tenderloin, trimmed
1 tablespoon vegetable oil
Orange Curry Sauce (at right)

Combine the molasses, soy sauce, curry base and gingerroot in a 9×13-inch baking dish and mix well. Add the pork and turn to coat. Marinate in the refrigerator for 1 to 4 hours.

Remove the pork from the marinade; discard the marinade. Heat the oil in a large heavy ovenproof skillet over medium-high heat. Add the pork. Cook for 3 minutes per side or until browned.

Place the skillet in a 350-degree oven. Roast for 25 minutes or to 160 degrees on a meat thermometer. Remove the pork to a platter. Tent with foil to keep warm.

Cut the pork into 1-inch-thick slices. Serve with the Orange Curry Sauce.

Yield: 4 servings

ORANGE CURRY SAUCE

3 cups orange juice
1 carrot, chopped
2 tablespoons chopped cilantro
2 tablespoons grated gingerroot
2 garlic cloves, sliced
1 jalapeño chile, seeded, minced
1 tablespoon cumin
1 tablespoon Thai red curry base
6 tablespoons butter, cut into pieces
Salt and pepper to taste

Bring the first 8 ingredients to a boil in a saucepan. Boil until the carrot is tender and liquid is reduced by 1/2. Purée in batches in a blender; strain. Whisk the butter into the hot purée in a bowl. Season with salt and pepper.

CLASSIC BRUNSWICK STEW

1   pound ground beef
1   pound onions, chopped
2   (3-pound) chickens, cooked, chopped
1   pound pork, cooked, chopped
4   (14-ounce) cans tomatoes
8   cups chicken broth
6   pounds potatoes, cooked, diced
2   (14-ounce) cans cream-style corn
2   (15-ounce) cans each peas and butter beans
2   (14-ounce) bottles ketchup
3/4 cup Worcestershire sauce

Brown the ground beef with the onions in a Dutch oven, stirring until the ground beef is crumbly; drain. Add the chicken, pork, tomatoes and broth. Bring to a boil. Reduce the heat to low. Simmer for 30 minutes. Stir in the potatoes, corn, peas, beans, ketchup and Worcestershire sauce. Cook for 30 minutes or until the flavors are blended.

Yield: 16 servings

FISH BAKE CASSEROLE

1   pound flounder fillets
1   to 2 tablespoons lemon juice
    Salt and pepper to taste
3   or 4 large potatoes, sliced
3   or 4 large onions, sliced
8   ounces bacon

Season the fish lightly with lemon juice, salt and pepper. Place in a single layer in a shallow baking dish. Layer the potatoes and onions over the fish. Cover with the bacon. Bake at 350 degrees for 30 minutes or until the bacon is crisp, the potatoes are tender and the fish flakes easily.

Yield: 4 servings

CAULIFLOWER AU GRATIN

    2   tablespoons butter or margarine
    2   tablespoons flour
    3/4 cup fat-free chicken broth
    3/4 cup skim milk
    1   bay leaf
    1   garlic clove, halved
    1   cup shredded reduced-fat Cheddar cheese
         Salt and pepper to taste
    1   head cauliflower, cooked

Melt the butter in a saucepan. Add the flour, stirring until smooth. Stir in the broth and milk gradually. Add the bay leaf and garlic. Cook until thickened, stirring constantly. Remove and discard the bay leaf and garlic. Stir in the cheese until melted. Season with salt and pepper.

Separate the cauliflower into florets. Place in a 1-quart baking dish. Top with the cheese sauce. Bake at 400 degrees for 30 minutes.

Yield: 4 servings

CORI'S SWEET POTATOES

    1   (2-pound) can sweet potatoes, drained, sliced
    4   cups sliced apples
    3/4 cup maple syrup
    1/4 cup (1/2 stick) butter, melted
    1   teaspoon salt

Place the sweet potatoes and apples in a greased 9×13-inch baking dish.

Combine the maple syrup, butter and salt in a bowl and mix well. Pour over the sweet potatoes and apples. Cover with foil.

Bake at 350 degrees for 45 minutes. Uncover. Bake for 30 minutes longer.

Yield: 6 servings

As the season advances, residents and visitors enjoy a traditional tour of Tryon Palace, appreciating time-honored decorations of fresh fruit and greenery and the holiday aromas from confections and delicacies. The highlight of the season, the Christmas Candlelight Tours, feature hundreds of candles illuminating the palace and the historical homes ornamented as they have been for generations.

SALLY LUNN BREAD

1   cup milk
1/2 cup shortening
1/4 cup water
1 1/3 cups sifted flour
1/3 cup sugar
2   teaspoons salt
2   envelopes dry yeast
2/3 cup sifted flour
3   eggs
2   cups sifted flour

Heat the milk, shortening and water to 120 degrees in a saucepan. (The shortening does not need to melt.)

Combine 1 1/3 cups flour, sugar, salt and yeast in a large mixing bowl. Add the warm milk mixture. Beat at medium speed for about 2 minutes, scraping down the side of the bowl occasionally. Add 2/3 cup flour and eggs gradually. Beat at high speed for 2 minutes. Add 2 cups flour and mix well. (The batter will be thick, but not stiff.)

Cover and let rise in a warm, draft-free place for 1 1/4 hours or until doubled in bulk.

Beat the dough down with a spatula or at low speed with an electric mixer. Spoon into a greased 10-inch tube or bundt pan. Cover and let rise in a warm, draft-free place for 30 minutes or until increased in bulk by 1/2 to 1/3.

Bake at 350 degrees for 40 to 50 minutes. Run a knife around the center and edge of the pan. Invert the bread onto a plate and cool.

Yield: 16 servings

RICH TWELFTH NIGHT CAKE

2   cups (4 sticks) butter, softened
1   cup packed brown sugar
9   eggs
1   cup packed brown sugar
3¹/2 cups flour
2   teaspoons mace
2   teaspoons cinnamon
1   teaspoon baking soda
3   pounds currants
2   pounds raisins, cut into small pieces
³/4   cup blanched almonds, chopped

Cream the butter and 1 cup brown sugar in a mixing bowl until light and fluffy. Add the eggs 1 at a time, mixing well after each addition. Beat until the mixture is thick and pale yellow. Fold in 1 cup brown sugar.

Sift the flour, mace, cinnamon and baking soda into a large bowl. Stir in the currants, raisins and almonds. Add to the butter mixture and mix well.

Line two 5×9-inch loaf pans with waxed paper that has been buttered on both sides. Spoon the batter into the pans, filling each about ²/3 full.

Bake at 275 degrees for 3¹/2 to 4 hours or until the surface of the cake feels firm and springs back when pressed. Run a knife around the sides of the pans. Cool the cakes in the pans. Remove from the pans to serve.

Yield: 24 servings

Twelfth Night cake was traditionally served in England and the colonies on the feast of Epiphany, the last of the twelve days of Christmas. It was a spicy plum cake with a hard white icing. Earlier traditions called for a bean and a pea to be baked into the cake. If a gentleman was served the slice of cake with the bean inside, he was declared king for the evening and the host of next year's ball. When a lady was served the pea, she became the queen and had the honor of baking next year's cake!

ANGEL BARS

1 (22-ounce) can pie
   filling (any flavor)
1 package angel food
   cake mix
   Chopped pecans
   (optional)
   Flaked coconut
   (optional)
   Confectioners'
   sugar (optional)

Combine the pie filling
and cake mix in a bowl
and mix well. Spoon
into a greased 9×13-
inch baking pan. Top
with pecans and
coconut. Bake at 350
degrees for 30 minutes
or until the bars test
done. Cool in the
pan on a wire rack.
Sprinkle with
confectioners' sugar.
Cut into bars.

$\mathcal{E}$ULA'S CAKE

11   egg whites
3   cups sifted flour
1   teaspoon baking powder
1/2 teaspoon salt
1 1/4 cups sugar
11   egg yolks
1 1/4 cups sugar
2   cups (4 sticks) unsalted butter, softened
2   teaspoons vanilla extract
2   tablespoons water

Place the egg whites in a large mixing bowl. Let stand at room temperature for 1 hour.

Sift the flour, baking powder and salt together; set aside.

Beat the egg whites until foamy. Add 1 1/4 cups sugar, 1/4 cup at a time, beating well after each addition. Beat until soft peaks form. Gently spoon egg whites into a medium bowl.

Beat the egg yolks, 1 1/4 cups sugar, butter, vanilla and water in the same mixing bowl at high speed for 5 minutes or until light and fluffy. Add the dry ingredients and beat at low speed just until well mixed. Beat in 1/2 of the egg whites at low speed gradually. Fold in the remaining egg whites. Pour into a well-greased and floured 10-inch tube pan.

Bake at 350 degrees for 1 hour and 5 minutes or until a wooden pick inserted near the center comes out clean. Cool in the pan for 15 minutes. Remove from the pan to a wire rack to cool completely. To serve, cut into thin slices.

Yield: 30 servings

HOLIDAY CHOCOLATE NUT SQUARES

1/2 cup (1 stick) butter or margarine, softened
1/4 cup sugar
1 1/4 cups flour
1/2 cup sugar
1/4 cup (1/2 stick) butter or margarine
2 tablespoons heavy cream
1 3/4 cups pecans or walnuts, coarsely chopped
1 cup flaked coconut
4 ounces semisweet chocolate, coarsely chopped

Beat 1/2 cup butter and 1/4 cup sugar in a mixing bowl until light and fluffy. Blend in the flour. Press over the bottom of a 9-inch square baking pan. Bake at 350 degrees for 18 minutes or until the edges are lightly browned; set aside.

Heat 1/2 cup sugar, 1/4 cup butter and cream in a saucepan until the butter melts and the mixture is blended, stirring constantly. Stir in the pecans; set aside.

Sprinkle the coconut and chocolate over the baked crust. Top with the pecan mixture. Bake at 350 degrees for 20 minutes or until golden brown. Cool in the pan on a wire rack. Cut into squares.

Yield: 16 servings

BROWN SUGAR FUDGE

1   *cup packed brown sugar*
1   *cup sugar*
1   *tablespoon baking cocoa*
$1/2$ *cup milk*
2   *tablespoons peanut butter*
1   *tablespoon butter*
1   *teaspoon vanilla extract*

Combine the brown sugar, sugar, baking cocoa, milk and peanut butter in a saucepan. Cook over medium heat to 234 to 240 degrees on a candy thermometer, soft-ball stage. Add the butter and vanilla.

Place the pan in a bowl of cold water. Beat until thick. Pour into an 8-inch square pan. Refrigerate until firm.

Yield: 32 servings

ENGLISH TRIFLE

5   egg yolks
2   cups milk, scalded
3/4   cup sugar
3   tablespoons flour
1   tablespoon butter
1   teaspoon vanilla extract
2   (3-ounce) packages plain ladyfingers
1/4   cup dry sherry
2   (10-ounce) packages frozen raspberries, thawed, drained
1   pint whipping cream
      Confectioners' sugar to taste

Beat the egg yolks in the top of a double boiler. Add the hot milk slowly, whisking constantly. Combine the sugar and flour in a bowl and mix well. Whisk into the egg mixture until smooth. Cook over simmering water until the custard is thickened and coats a metal spoon with a thin film. Add the butter and vanilla and mix well. Cool.

Split the ladyfingers into halves. Line the bottom and side of a trifle dish or glass serving bowl with the ladyfingers. Brush with sherry. Top with a thin layer of custard, the raspberries and the remaining custard. Drizzle with sherry.

Beat the whipping cream in a mixing bowl until stiff, adding enough confectioners' sugar to sweeten lightly. Spread over the top of the trifle.

Yield: 10 servings

The families of New Bern decorate their homes with innovative and traditional displays of Christmas lights and characters. The glow of Christmas lights against winter's dark landscape embodies the excitement of the season. Whether attending a production of Handel's *Messiah*, decorating Christmas trees, or watching children perform in local Christmas pageants, each family adds the experiences of a Coastal Carolina Christmas to its album of memories every year.

Summer had arrived early that year. It was hot…and it was crowded. Two people passed out from the heat. But what better place to get ill?

It was April 22, 1963. Craven County Hospital was to be formally dedicated. This was, indeed, an historic day. Health care in Craven County was about to change dramatically…and it hasn't stopped changing since.

A few years earlier, a New Bern physician, Dr. Dale Millns, and town community leaders Larry B. Pate and Robert Stallings, identified the crucial need in this area for one full-service hospital. After convincing the county commissioners of the critical need, the Craven County Hospital Corporation was formed and purchased the 75-bed St. Luke's Hospital from the Sisters of Saint Joseph who had run it as a private facility for many years. The purchase price for the building and all equipment was $55,000.

Under the Hill-Burton Act, however, Craven County's population was not great enough to justify the 100 beds the county wanted. Recognizing that Craven's neighboring counties were without a hospital as well, the population bases of Jones and Pamlico Counties were used to reach the 100-bed mark. The old prison site on the Kinston Highway was given to the county by then Governor Luther Hodges. Construction began.

On April 22, 1963, the need was met, the dream realized. Residents of Craven, Jones, and Pamlico now had their own modern, 100-bed hospital. Total cost of the new facility, equipment included, was $2.1 million. The daily rate for a private room was $18.00.

That was 38 years and 213 beds ago.

Today, Craven Health Care has grown beyond the perimeter of the old prison site, reaching as far west as Vanceboro. The 313-bed Craven Regional Medical Center, a full-service acute-care facility, still occupies the prison site; however, Craven Health Care, committed to meeting the ever-increasing, rapidly evolving, health care needs of its region, has branched out and positioned itself well for the future. In addition to the medical center, Craven Health Care encompasses Craven Diagnostic Center and Craven Surgery Center, two freestanding facilities providing outpatient care. Also included are Coastal Rehabilitation Center, a 20-bed inpatient rehabilitation unit, 100-bed Twin Rivers Nursing Center, Craven Medical Supply, Craven Home Care, and Craven Primary Care located in western Craven County.

In 1999, over 13,000 patients were admitted to the medical center; 60,000 outpatient procedures were completed; 10,873 surgical procedures were performed; 33,103 people were cared for in the emergency department; and Home Care made over 16,881 visits to area homes, providing quality health care in the most comfortable of settings.

The county's third-largest employer, Craven Health Care boasts a staff of 1300-plus medical and support personnel, with a payroll of over $42 million. Over 180 physicians representing most medical specialties prescribe the care delivered at the medical center and its subsidiaries. Comprehensive cardiac care including surgery, state-of-the-art cancer treatment, and rehabilitation are among the organization's centers of excellence. Craven is unsurpassed locally in the outpatient services arena–the future of health care.

With few exceptions, Craven Health Care has touched the lives of almost every family in this region.

CONTRIBUTORS LIST

Jo Aiken

Nancy Alexander

Meredith Andrews

Sandra Andrews

Jeanette Avery

Nat Baggett

Mary Barden

Nora Barden

Jean H. Barker

Chanell Barksdale

Belinda Barr

Alice Barrett

Joni Battersby

Leah Bell

Anne Bennett

Beth Benson, M.D.

Pauline Blair

Joanne Boyle

Laura M. Brauninger

Marie Breitfeller

Janet Buff

Roy Burris

Ann Bustard

Celia Byrd

Trish Callison

Constance Carluccio

Claudia E. Casey

Betty Cashwell

Loretta Croscutt

Sherry Cuthrell

Diane Dail

Mike Davis

Luz A. Dehunt

Robi Delk

Mollie Doyle

Teri Duckworth

Maxine Dunbar

Lisa Edwards

Faye Erichsen

Lynn Everett

Nancy Everett

Dianne Ezell

Angie Farmer

Beverely Fitzgerald

Karen Frank

Kittie Ann Franklin

Shirley Gage

Cathy Garvick

Colleen Gaskins

Jenny Godwin

Anne Goldman

Carla Gray

Robert "Cody" Griffith

Marta Shultz Grubb

Ginger Gunsten

Annie Hall

Roberta Hand

Linda Hanlon

Esther H. Hardison

Kathi Hardison

Judie Harriet

Judith Hartman-Bell

Betsy Hathaway

Hatteras Yachts

Madonna Hawks

Ellen Hawley

Ann Healy, M.D.

Michelle Hicks

Anne Hiller

Tina Holton

Nancy Hunt

Janice Ipock

Barbara C. Jackson

Susie Jarman

Dawn Jenkins

Faye Johnson	Anna Norris	Beth Smith
Deborah Joyner	Lisa Norton	Tracy Stanley
Margaret Lamb	Jackie Pajak	Wanda Stigar
Julie Lansdowne	Tryon Palace	Barbara Stocks
Susan Lasater	Bud Parker	Donna Nelson Stocks
Wendy Lee	Dr. Rob and Martha Ann	Tracy Stohrer
Dianne Lewis	Patterson	Lisa Sugg
Judy Lewis	Warren Phillips	RoseMarie Suhrie
Sam K. Lewis	Judy Pierce	Deborah Sutton
Sandie Maher	Leslie Pittman	Carol Taylor
Lynn Maletzky	Rhonda Potter	Ramona H. Thomas
Megan McGarvey	Nadine Rhodes	Sharon Thompson
Sue McKain	Ann Robertson	Alice G. Underhill
Georgia H. McKenzie	Debra Lee Roelofs	Lea F. Vary
Marcelene McLure	Lynne Rousseau	Beth Wagner
Bettina Meekins, M.D.	Vickie Rowe	Teresa Warren
Roberta Milford	Vicky W. Saulter	Cheryl A. Watson
Annette Mills	Linda Sawyer	Vicky W. Waulter
Mary Mooring	Lou Ann Schroeder	Karla E. Weatherly
Alison G. Moritz	Evelyn Scott	Nina Wells
Kenneth E. Morris, Jr.	Patricia H. Scott	Lorri Wetherington
Linda R. Morris	Stephanie Scott	Debra M. Kinsey White
Liz Murphy	Claire Shields	Linda T. Whitlock
Mary Nelson	Margaret Shields	Patty Willis
Janet Newman	Wright Shields, M.D.	Helen Zak

INDEX

Accompaniments
Green Tomato Relish, 100
Microwave Bread and Butter
Pickles, 100
Summery Minted Mango
Salsa, 79
Supper Club Pepper Pesto, 28
Watermelon Rind
Pickles, 100

Appetizers. *See also* Dips;
Spreads
Angels on Horseback, 77
Bacon-Cheese Fingers, 15
Beer Batter Shrimp, 126
Caponata, 150
Carolina Crab Cakes, 171
Chicken Salad Tartlets, 15
Chicken Wraps, 45
Do-Dads, 151
Feta Cheese Bites, 126
Grilled Shrimp Appetizer, 67
Hot Cheese Puffs, 184
Layered Seafood Tray, 78
Nancy's Chipped Beef, 27
Paprika Chips, 28
Quick and Easy Pinwheels, 14
Sausage and Cheese Puffs, 162
Smoked Oyster Pâté, 149
Stuffed Mushrooms, 27
Tasty Chicken Wings, 125

Apples
Apple Crumb Pie, 123
Apple Raisin Pork Chops, 141
Applesauce Cake, 133
Apple Topping, 22
Autumn Tossed Salad, 138
Cori's Sweet Potatoes, 191
Cranberry Apple
Casserole, 144

Homemade Applesauce, 133
Roast Pork with Brie and
Apples, 175

Artichokes
Chicken and Artichokes, 34
Hot Artichoke Dip, 46
Louisiana Crayfish Boil, 85

Asparagus
Green Salad with Asparagus,
Orange and Red Onion, 32
Sesame Asparagus, 88

Bananas
Nutty Banana Bread, 21
Strawberry Smoothie, 14

Beans
Back Porch Black Bean and
Monterey Jack Cheese
Casserole, 72
Black Dog Chicken Chili, 47
Chicken, Beans and Greens
Soup, 29
Chili, 164
Classic Brunswick Stew, 190
Confetti Corn, 89
Hot Cheddar Bean Dip, 163
Lentil Soup, 127
Pantry Soup, 164
Phillips' Filthy Rice, 119
Seasoned Black Beans, 72
Speedy Black Bean
Soup, 30

Beef. *See also* Ground Beef
Grilled Beef Tenderloin
Tips, 50
Hatteras Meat Loaf, 139
London Broil, 83

Marinated Roast Beef, 188
McStroganoff, 128
Mostaccioli, 33
Nancy's Chipped Beef, 27
Quick and Easy
Pinwheels, 14

Beverages
Barbara's Summer
Refresher, 66
Cap'n Polly's Eggnog, 183
Claire's Lemonade Stand
Lemonade, 66
Fish House Punch, 77
Strawberry Smoothie, 14
Tropicana Punch, 125

Blueberries
Blueberry Pie, 103
Max's Blueberry Crisp, 74

Breads
Feather-Light Dumplings, 176
Hatteras Baked Pancake, 22
Pumpkin Bread, 145
Sally Lunn Bread, 192

Breads, Loaves
Boston Brown Bread, 168
Easy Italian Bread, 39
Grandpa's Homemade
Bread, 40
Irish Soda Bread, 121
Nanny's Date Nut
Bread, 154
Nutty Banana Bread, 21

Broccoli
Broccoli Cheese Soup, 94
Broccoli Salad, 94
Broccoli Supreme, 38

Brunch
Breakfast Casserole, 17
Breakfast Pizza, 17
Crab Quiche, 18

Cakes
Applesauce Cake, 133
Carrot Cake, 102
Chocolate Almond Cake, 23
Chocolate Chip Cake, 169
Chocolate Lover's Cake, 41
Delicious Pound Cake, 154
Eula's Cake, 194
Hot Fudge Pudding Cake, 146
Orange Raisin Cake, 122
Piña Colada Cake, 74
Poppy Seed Cake, 91
Rich Twelfth Night
    Cake, 193
Strawberry Cake, 75
Super Seven-Up Cake, 179

Carrots
Broccoli Cheese Soup, 94
Broccoli Salad, 94
Carrot Cake, 102
Chicken, Beans and Greens
    Soup, 29
Chicken Vegetable
    Soup, 173
Grilled Summer
    Vegetables, 101
Grilled Vegetable Salad, 95
Hunter's Stew, 115
Lentil Soup, 127
Sesame Coleslaw, 96
Spicy Sesame and Ginger
    Noodle Salad, 80
Sweet-and-Sour Meatballs, 51
Tangy Marinated Carrots, 55
Venison Ham, 112

Cauliflower
Broccoli Salad, 94
Cauliflower au Gratin, 191
Cauliflower Italiano, 88

Chicken
Black Dog Chicken
    Chili, 47
Chicken and Artichokes, 34
Chicken, Beans and Greens
    Soup, 29
Chicken Casserole, 177
Chicken Enchiladas, 167
Chicken Fiesta, 130
Chicken Salad Tartlets, 15
Chicken Vegetable Soup, 173
Chicken with Feather-Light
    Dumplings, 176
Chicken Wraps, 45
Classic Brunswick Stew, 190
Crispy Golden Chicken, 152
Diane's Nutty Chicken, 97
Kiwi, Strawberry and
    Chicken Salad, 174
Low Country Jambalaya, 37
Mustard Herb Chicken, 97
Sesame Chicken with
    Bow Tie Pasta, 163
Tasty Chicken Wings, 125

Chocolate
Brown Sugar Fudge, 196
Chocolate Almond Cake, 23
Chocolate Almond Icing, 23
Chocolate Buttercream
    Frosting, 41
Chocolate Chip Cake, 169
Chocolate Éclair, 179
Chocolate Lover's Cake, 41
Chocolate Oatmeal
    Cookies, 155

Holiday Chocolate Nut
    Squares, 195
Hot Fudge Pudding
    Cake, 146
No-Bake Cookies, 147
Sinful Chocolate Pie, 123
To-Die-For Chocolate Pecan
    Pie, 58
Trophy Cookies, 59

Clams
Bretagne Bouillabaisse, 186
Clam Dip, 149
Down East Clam
    Chowder, 110

Cookies
Chocolate Oatmeal
    Cookies, 155
Hole-in-One Peanut Butter
    Cookies, 60
Italian Twists, 155
Meringues Chantilly, 43
No-Bake Cookies, 147
Oatmeal Raisin Cookies, 156
Seafoam Cookies, 91
Trophy Cookies, 59

Corn
Broccoli Supreme, 38
Classic Brunswick Stew, 190
Confetti Corn, 89
Corn Casserole, 143
Corn Pudding, 56
Louisiana Crayfish Boil, 85
Pantry Soup, 164
Speedy Black Bean Soup, 30
Tasty Chicken Wings, 125

Crab Meat
Carolina Crab Cakes, 171

Carolina Crab Meat
  Appetizer, 67
Cody's Seafood Gumbo
  "Louisiana Style," 53
Crab Cakes with Chardonnay
  Cream Sauce, 84
Crab Quiche, 18
Hot Crab Dip, 185
Layered Seafood Tray, 78
Margaret Dolan's Crab Meat
  Imperial, 35
Seafood Thermidor, 87

Cranberries
Cranberry Apple
  Casserole, 144
Cranberry Orange
  Stuffing, 141
Cranberry Salad, 187
Mixed Green Salad with
  Roquefort Vinaigrette, 187

Crust, Spiced Nut, 134

Desserts. *See also* Cakes;
  Cookies; Pies
Angel Bars, 194
Brown Sugar Fudge, 196
Chocolate Éclair, 179
Easy Orange Sherbet, 75
English Trifle, 197
Fruit Dip, 180
Ginger Cointreau Sherbet, 42
Guilt-Free Cheesecake, 25
Holiday Chocolate Nut
  Squares, 195
Homemade Applesauce, 133
Lemon Squares, 24
Max's Blueberry Crisp, 74
Orange Balls, 169
Peanut Brittle, 180

Pecan Tasties, 135
Praline Pecan Crunch, 168
Spanish Cream, 181
Zany Zucchini Bars, 104

Dips
Carolina Crab Meat
  Appetizer, 67
Clam Dip, 149
Dill Vegetable Dip, 93
Dip for Raw Vegetables, 93
Fruit Dip, 180
Hot Artichoke Dip, 46
Hot Cheddar Bean Dip, 163
Hot Crab Dip, 185
Seven-Layer Dip, 79
Spicy Chili Cheese Dip, 162
Spinach Bacon Dip, 16

Fish. *See also* Salmon
Bretagne Bouillabaisse, 186
Cape Lookout Baked
  Flounder, 69
Fish Bake Casserole, 190
Golden Catfish Fillets, 52
Island Grilled Swordfish, 83

Frostings
Chocolate Buttercream
  Frosting, 41
Cream Cheese Frosting, 102
Strawberry Frosting, 75

Fruit. *See* Apples; Bananas;
  Blueberries; Cranberries;
  Pineapple; Strawberries

Game Birds
Cornish Hens with Currant
  Sauce, 115
Dove Pie, 116

Duck and Walnut Salad, 111
Pheasant with Scotch
  Whiskey, 118

Grains
Back Porch Black Bean and
  Monterey Jack Cheese
  Casserole, 72
Curried Rice, 38
Hot Chopped Spinach
  Casserole, 165
Low Country Jambalaya, 37
Low Country Shrimp and
  Grits, 36
Phillips' Filthy Rice, 119
Rice Oriental, 89

Ground Beef
Chili, 164
Classic Brunswick Stew, 190
Georgia Bird's Spaghetti
  Sauce, 129
Hamburger Casserole, 175
Hatteras Meat Loaf, 139
Hot Chopped Spinach
  Casserole, 165
Pantry Soup, 164
Sloppy Joes, 152
Sweet-and-Sour
  Meatballs, 51
Three Shepherds' Pie, 188

Icings
Chocolate Almond Icing, 23
Cream Cheese Icing, 169

Lamb Chops, Grilled, 69

Lobster
Bretagne Bouillabaisse, 186
Seafood Thermidor, 87

Marinades
  Beach Marinade, 83
  Fish Marinade, 70
  Mustard Herb Marinade, 97

Mushrooms
  Caesar Salad with Portobello
    Mushrooms, 31
  Chicken and Artichokes, 34
  Frisée, Radicchio and Mixed
    Greens with Shrimp, 82
  Georgia Bird's Spaghetti
    Sauce, 129
  Holiday Oyster Stew, 137
  Hot Chopped Spinach
    Casserole, 165
  Louisiana Crayfish Boil, 85
  McStroganoff, 128
  Phillips' Filthy Rice, 119
  Portobello Mushroom
    Sandwiches with Rosemary
    Aïoli, 153
  Seafarer's Delight, 185
  Seafood Thermidor, 87
  Shrimp Chippewa Soup, 16
  Stuffed Mushrooms, 27
  Venison Medallions with
    Creamy Mushroom
    Sauce, 114

Oysters
  Angels on Horseback, 77
  Holiday Oyster Stew, 137
  Scalloped Oysters, 119
  Smoked Oyster Pâté, 149

Pasta
  Baked Macaroni and
    Cheese, 178
  Chicken, Beans and Greens
    Soup, 29

  Chicken Vegetable Soup, 173
  Hamburger Casserole, 175
  McStroganoff, 128
  Mostaccioli, 33
  Pantry Soup, 164
  Penne with Tomatoes, Olives
    and Two Cheeses, 98
  Sesame Chicken with
    Bow Tie Pasta, 163
  Shrimp Tortellini, 86
  Spicy Sesame and Ginger
    Noodle Salad, 80
  Spinach Lasagna, 99
  Tortellini Salad with
    Vegetables, 151

Peas
  Black-Eyed Pea Hoppin'
    John, 54
  Eighteen-Hole Salad, 49
  Spicy Sesame and Ginger
    Noodle Salad, 80
  Spring Pea Salad, 49
  Tortellini Salad with
    Vegetables, 151

Pies
  Apple Crumb Pie, 123
  Blueberry Pie, 103
  Caribbean Coconut
    Cream Pie, 90
  Pumpkin Pie, 134
  Sinful Chocolate Pie, 123
  Strawberry Rhubarb Pie, 103
  Sweet Potato Pie, 147
  To-Die-For Chocolate
    Pecan Pie, 58

Pineapple
  Celebration Glazed Ham, 174
  Cranberry Salad, 187

  Creamy Orange Pineapple
    Salad, 68
  Easy Orange Sherbet, 75
  Pineapple Casserole, 18
  Sweet-and-Sour Meatballs, 51
  Tasty Chicken Wings, 125

Pork. *See also* Sausage
  Apple Raisin Pork
    Chops, 141
  BBQ Spareribs with
    Homemade Barbecue
    Sauce, 166
  Celebration Glazed Ham, 174
  Classic Brunswick Stew, 190
  Crown Pork Roast with
    Cranberry Orange
    Stuffing, 140
  Hatteras Meat Loaf, 139
  Roast Pork with Brie and
    Apples, 175
  Saucy Pork Chops, 130
  Thai-Spiced Pork Tenderloin
    with Orange Curry
    Sauce, 189

Potatoes
  Cape Lookout Baked
    Flounder, 69
  Classic Brunswick Stew, 190
  Down East Clam
    Chowder, 110
  Fish Bake Casserole, 190
  German Potato Salad, 131
  Green Onion Potato
    Casserole, 73
  Hash Brown Potato
    Casserole, 19
  Herb-Roasted Potatoes
    Poupon, 120
  Hunter's Stew, 115

Louisiana Crayfish Boil, 85
Mashed Potatoes, 177
Rosemary Potatoes, 56
Three Shepherds' Pie, 188

Poultry. *See* Chicken;
  Game Birds; Turkey

Salad Dressings
  Broccoli Salad Dressing, 94
  Buttermilk Dressing, 32
  Carolina Peanut
    Vinaigrette, 138
  Italian Dressing, 138
  Italian Salad Dressing, 88
  Poppy Seed Dressing, 174

Salads
  Autumn Tossed Salad, 138
  Broccoli Salad, 94
  Caesar Salad with Portobello
    Mushrooms, 31
  Cranberry Salad, 187
  Creamy Orange Pineapple
    Salad, 68
  Duck and Walnut Salad, 111
  Eighteen-Hole Salad, 49
  Frisée, Radicchio and Mixed
    Greens with Shrimp, 82
  Green Salad with Asparagus,
    Orange and Red Onion, 32
  Grilled Vegetable Salad, 95
  Kiwi, Strawberry and
    Chicken Salad, 174
  Mixed Green Salad with
    Roquefort Vinaigrette, 187
  Sesame Chicken with
    Bow Tie Pasta, 163
  Sesame Coleslaw, 96
  Spicy Sesame and Ginger
    Noodle Salad, 80

Spring Pea Salad, 49
Strawberry Pretzel Salad, 81
Tortellini Salad with
  Vegetables, 151

Salmon
  Grilled Salmon with Lemon
    Caper Sauce, 70
  Honey Ginger Salmon, 131

Sauces, Savory
  Chardonnay Cream
    Sauce, 84
  Currant Sauce, 115
  Homemade Barbecue
    Sauce, 166
  Orange Curry Sauce, 189
  Remoulade Sauce, 172
  Rosemary Aïoli, 153
  Wild Game Sauce, 119

Sausage
  Breakfast Casserole, 17
  Breakfast Pizza, 17
  Cranberry Orange
    Stuffing, 141
  Hot Chopped Spinach
    Casserole, 165
  Hunter's Stew, 115
  Louisiana Crayfish
    Boil, 85
  Phillips' Filthy Rice, 119
  Sausage and Cheese
    Puffs, 162
  Spicy Chili Cheese
    Dip, 162
  Stuffed Mushrooms, 27

Scallops
  Bretagne Bouillabaisse, 186
  Seafarer's Delight, 185

Seafood. *See also* Clams;
    Crab Meat; Lobster;
    Oysters; Scallops; Shrimp
  Louisiana Crayfish Boil, 85

Shrimp
  Beer Batter Shrimp, 126
  Cody's Seafood Gumbo
    "Louisiana Style," 53
  Frisée, Radicchio and Mixed
    Greens with Shrimp, 82
  Grilled Shrimp Appetizer, 67
  Layered Seafood Tray, 78
  Low Country Jambalaya, 37
  Low Country Shrimp and
    Grits, 36
  New Orleans Shrimp
    Creole, 71
  Seafood Thermidor, 87
  Shrimp au Gratin, 117
  Shrimp Chippewa Soup, 16
  Shrimp Tortellini, 86

Side Dishes
  Cranberry Apple
    Casserole, 144
  Cranberry Orange
    Stuffing, 141
  Dumplings with
    Sauerkraut, 132
  Pineapple Casserole, 18

Soups
  Black Dog Chicken
    Chili, 47
  Bretagne Bouillabaisse, 186
  Broccoli Cheese Soup, 94
  Chicken, Beans and Greens
    Soup, 29
  Chicken Vegetable Soup, 173
  Chili, 164

Down East Clam
    Chowder, 110
Egg Drop Soup, 48
Fish Stock, 186
Holiday Oyster Stew, 137
Lentil Soup, 127
Making Shrimp Stock, 53
Pantry Soup, 164
Seafarer's Delight, 185
Shrimp Chippewa Soup, 16
Speedy Black Bean Soup, 30
Tomato Herb Soup, 127

Spinach
Chicken Vegetable Soup, 173
Hot Chopped Spinach
    Casserole, 165
Michelle's Spinach Pie, 20
Pickett Duffy's Spinach
    Soufflé, 178
Sesame Coleslaw, 96
Spinach Bacon Dip, 16
Spinach Lasagna, 99

Spreads
Christmas Cheese Ball, 184
Onion Bread Spread, 46

Squash
Grilled Summer
    Vegetables, 101
Grilled Vegetable Salad, 95
Muriel Gray's Squash
    Casserole, 57
Vegetable Pudding, 132

Strawberries
Guilt-Free Cheesecake, 25
Kiwi, Strawberry and
    Chicken Salad, 174
Strawberry Cake, 75
Strawberry Frosting, 75
Strawberry Pretzel Salad, 81
Strawberry Rhubarb Pie, 103
Strawberry Smoothie, 14

Sweet Potatoes
Cori's Sweet Potatoes, 191
Southern-Style Sweet
    Potatoes, 144
Sweet Potato Pie, 147

Toppings
Apple Topping, 22
Coconut Topping, 122
Crumb Topping, 123

Turkey
Low Country Jambalaya, 37
Yacht Club Turkey, 142

Vegetables. *See also* Artichokes;
    Asparagus; Beans;
    Broccoli; Carrots;
    Cauliflower; Corn;
    Mushrooms; Peas;
    Potatoes; Spinach; Squash;
    Sweet Potatoes; Zucchini
Caponata, 150
Chicken, Beans and Greens
    Soup, 29

Chicken Wraps, 45
Cody's Seafood Gumbo
    "Louisiana Style," 53
Dumplings with
    Sauerkraut, 132
Granddaddy's Collards, 143
Grilled Vegetable Salad, 95
Sesame Coleslaw, 96
Three Shepherds' Pie, 188
Tortellini Salad with
    Vegetables, 151

Venison
All-Day Deer Roast, 113
Hunter's Stew, 115
Venison Ham, 112
Venison Medallions with
    Creamy Mushroom
    Sauce, 114

Zucchini
Grilled Summer
    Vegetables, 101
Grilled Vegetable Salad, 95
Stewed Tomatoes, Squash and
    Onion, 101
Tortellini Salad with
    Vegetables, 151
Zany Zucchini Bars, 104

ORDER INFORMATION

CRMC Foundation
P. O. Box 12157
New Bern, NC 28561
(252) 633-8247

Sponsored by

JENKINS
The Energy Company

Pollocksville
Richlands
New Bern
Bayboro
Morehead City
Swansboro
Jacksonville
Pink Hill
Warsaw
Mt. Olive
Beulaville
Goldsboro
Fayetteville
Wilson
Greenville
Wilmington
Burgaw
(Four County Propane)
Angier (Garner Gas)
Kill Devil Hills
(Owens Gas)
Merry Hill
(Quality Gas Service)

Name   (Please print)

Street Address

City   State   Zip

Telephone

Your Order	Qty	Total
Savoring the Seasons: Riverside $21.95 per book		$
NC residents add 6% sales tax at $1.32 per book		$
Shipping and handling $5.00 per book		$
Total		$

Method of Payment: [   ] VISA   [   ] MasterCard

[   ] Check payable to CRMC Foundation

Account Number   Expiration Date

Cardholder Name   (Please print)

Signature